The Joy of Selling

Also by Steve Chandler

The Joy
of Selling

Breakthrough ideas that
lead to success in sales

Steve Chandler

Robert D. Reed Publishers
Bandon, Oregon

Robert D. Reed Publishers
P.O. Box 1992
Bandon, OR 97411
Phone: 541-347-9882 • Fax: 541-347-9883
E-mail: 4bobreed@msn.com
Web site: www.rdrpublishers.com

Designed and typeset by Katherine Hyde
Cover designed by Grant Prescott

ISBN 1-931741-58-1

Library of Congress Control Number: 2002095083

Produced and Printed in the United States of America

To Steve Hardison

Contents

1 Shine Your Mind on Your Goals

Ain't no sunshine when it's gone.

What is it? Your most important asset: your attention.

Where is your attention today? Where are you directing the light of your mind? On yourself? On your problems?

Or on the results you want to produce today?

Your mind is a beam of sun. The business world is a wet and shimmering garden of damp dark soil hiding so many seeds that are just waiting to grow. Wherever you turn your attention, that's where a flower will begin to grow.

My friend Jim Blasingame hosts a popular nationwide radio show called *The Small Business Advocate*. He recently told me that the first year he was on the air with his show he directed all his attention to the worries and problems of the show ... and the show really struggled. The next three years he began to pay more and more attention to the audience ... and the *audience* grew! Whatever he put his attention on would *grow*.

Anything you pay attention to expands. It grows. Pay attention to your house plants and they grow. Pay attention to your favorite sport, and your passion for that sport grows. Attention is like that. Anywhere you point it, the object of that attention grows.

Watch what happens when you pay a lot of attention to new opportunities for sales.

2   Make Some Friends in Low Places

By now, everyone's already told you to go high up. Sell to decision-makers in high places in the companies you are targeting.

You might even get lessons in "How to Get Past the Gatekeeper."

But whenever you talk to the person leading the team in sales, they will also have stories about the power of having friends in low places.

Even if you don't have an appointment with the big boss, and you someday would like one, it doesn't hurt to go by and meet the other people. Treat them all like gold. They *are* gold. They can tell you so much about the company they work for.

Once I got to know a woman named Marie who was out at the front desk of an enormous company I wanted to sell to. The more I stopped by and the more we talked, the more she felt like helping me. Finally one day she said, "Come by very early Saturday morning. She [the big boss] comes in at about seven and works for an hour or two. She's casual on Saturday and very open to seeing anyone who drops by. I'll meet you here and introduce you. We'll make it look relaxed and casual."

That one gesture led to my getting a lot of business. Marie had told me so much about the company that when I finally got to visit with Mrs. High Places, I was able to talk to her in her own language about the world she lives in. She immediately trusted me because of the obvious "research" I had done on her company. Research? Marie was my research.

There are no unimportant people. Everyone is a piece in the puzzle of life. Everyone plays a very important part. Everyone has power.

Your friends in low places have more interesting kinds of power than the higher executives because it's secret power. It's like a wizard's power. It's power they have stashed away in secret compartments. They have ways through the gate that they don't show to just anybody. And they will *never* show off their secret power until they trust you. It's that secret. And your competitors will never even know that this power exists because your competitors are learning how to *avoid* these people in low places and blast their way right to the top.

Your competitors are sitting in seminars learning how to get past the gatekeeper. How to get past Marie!

3   Guide Them
Toward the Dream

Lunita was a salesperson who realized she sold more once she learned to analyze dreams.

Lunita would ask, "What do you want? What is your dream? What would you love to see happen in your business?"

Then, finding out what the answers to these questions were, Lunita (being the masterful salesperson she was) promised to play her small part in bringing that dream into reality.

"I promise I will help you," she would say. "I will help you get what you intend to have. I will focus all of my actions and all my thinking on your goals. My office machines I am selling you will play an important part in that. They will make things more effective and more efficient for you around the office as you move toward your future. Your goals will be reached a little bit faster now."

Lunita led her team in sales.

4 Keep Using Your Courage

One of the great benefits and delights of selling is that it offers opportunities for courage. Not many professions do, so not many people ever go to their graves knowing how courageous they can really be.

As you decide, throughout the day, between two choices, any two choices, when you can't decide: pick the bravest choice.

Many times salespeople wonder how they could possibly do more work. They're becoming workaholics as it is. The answer is not in trying to do *more* work. The real quantum leaps come from doing *braver* work.

Think of ways throughout the day that you can do something bolder than usual. That will even *reduce* your work hours after awhile.

5 Train Yourself in Your Car

Today there are so many provocative and inspiring audio programs available for business women and men that driving to work can be one of the most useful times of the day.

Rather than trying to make a dozen badly communicated cell phone calls while driving, why not slide in a great tape or CD to listen to? Why not improve your business and marketing savvy every time you drive?

Cell phone calling and listening to the "news" on the radio can be a total waste of your driving time. It can increase your anxiety levels and make your day much more stressful than it needs to be. Make your phone calls when you are relaxed and confident and can communicate clearly and effectively, bringing your conversations to a warm and mature sense of completion.

You don't want your best prospective client to hear you talking this way:

"Hey, hi, thanks for taking my call . . . hold it! darn! I'm going under a BRIDGE?? #@$##@#@ oh MY WHAT THE? are you there? . . . yes I'm here, can you hear me? Sorry. I'm really sorry. Hold it. Gosh dang drivers today! Can you believe them? hello? hello? hello? I hate this phone . . . you? No, not you, the phone. I thought I had lost you. Anyway on the deal for November, hello? talk to me . . . oh my, my life is sh . . . Oh, YES! you're back? . . . hello . . . hello . . ."

This kind of call sends your client a simple message: your life is out of control.

Is that what you want to use your drive time for?

6 Enjoy Some Stage Fright

If you get stage fright before a big call, or before a big presentation, what does it mean? Does it mean you are a weak person? Does it mean you are unprepared? Does it mean you are immature?

No, it means none of those things.

It means you are in a truly great profession.

I mean, who else gets stage fright?

Great actors. Military heroes. Great athletes. Sometimes the prime minister of England, or the president of the United States. And *salespeople* about to participate in something big.

Stage fright doesn't mean anything negative about you. It means you are really living. You are about to challenge yourself again to perform when there is a lot at stake. You might be about to go somewhere you have never been before.

Most people can go years without any stage fright. Some, a lifetime. Why? Because they have cautiously worked their way underground into a safe haven of no-risk. They have figured out how to hide out from life. They live like shy worms under the soft wet soil of life.

The only problem with a life that has no stage fright in it is that it is not a life of adventure. You might get a mild sort of satisfaction in that life sometimes. But joy? No, there is no joy.

You need stage fright for joy. You can't live a hidden life and experience joy.

7 Produce Something

Words carry energy. Each word you say out loud or internally to yourself catalyzes a different response in your brain and therefore throughout your whole body. I always enjoy what happens when I increase the use of the word "produce."

If I want to move closer toward achieving my life's goals today, I might start my morning with the question, "What would I like to *produce* today?"

If I have a meeting with someone important, I might ask myself before going in, "What would I like this meeting to produce?"

Most people use the much weaker, "What do I hope will happen?"

If I think, always, about *producing* what I want, then I am constantly returning to my power base inside my mind. Do I want to produce an agreement? Do I want to produce a better relationship? Do I want to produce a whole new level of interest in how I can solve my prospect's problems? Do I want to produce a sale?

Two hours left in the day…what would I like to produce?

Not what "should" I be doing. But what will I *produce* right now. The words conjure up two different worlds altogether.

See what it's like to experience success that you yourself have produced for yourself. Produce relationships. Produce proposals. Produce trust. Don't simply hope these things will occur by themselves.

8 Stay in the Conversation

Reports over the years claim that the average salesperson spends just one-and-a-half hours a day selling. One-and-a-half hours! Those reports shock a lot of people who think they are spending the *whole day* selling.

The only real reason salespeople would let their selling time drop to that low a level would be ignorance. They are simply ignorant of when they are selling and when they are not. They have convinced themselves that everything they do all day is necessary, so therefore there is no way to add selling to the day without adding hours.

Not true.

Once you heighten your awareness of when you are selling and when you are not, you can find all kinds of ways to increase your selling time here and there. Every time you do, your income will increase too.

It all starts with your clear awareness of when you are in a *conversation*.

At any given moment in your day, you are either in a sales conversation or you are not. Your minutes each day can be accurately and precisely measured as either *in* or *out* of a conversation for a selling opportunity.

If you carried around a little beeper that went off at odd times and you had to jot down the words "in" or "out" every time it went off, based on whether at that very minute you were in a sales conversation, you would find out why you were succeeding or failing at sales.

People who fail in sales fail for one reason only: they stay outside of the conversation. They subconsciously don't want to be inside the conversation. Even though the conversation is where sales always occur.

Sales cannot happen *outside* of that conversation. No sale has ever occurred outside of a conversation.

You can learn to respect the power of the conversation. Learn to be drawn to it. You can learn to have conversation be all you move toward all day. Soon you might even find yourself feeling awkward whenever you are not in one. Let yourself feel that. It will lead to great things.

There is no middle area that you can be in. You are either in a conversation or you are not. If you are not, you will not sell. No sale can occur outside of one. Yet most salespeople have *no awareness* of all the time they spend outside of sales conversations. If they knew, they would be shocked.

The best way to produce this awareness and therefore heighten your sales performance is to track yourself: spend two experimental days logging each minute of your business day. Open up a little notebook. Whenever you go into a sales conversation, log in. When you stop the conversation, log out. Write down the time of day to the minute. At the end of the day add up your minutes. You might be surprised, at first. Unless you're currently leading the nation in sales, you might be surprised at how little time you spend inside the conversation that leads to sales.

Think of it like the old factory time clocks. You punch in when you're working, and you punch out when you stop.

Because if you really track this, the news is going to get good. Soon your heightened awareness will take you up into your spirit. You'll feel different when you're logged in. The more logged in you are, the more effective your day will feel. There will even be times when you feel like you've lived three days in a day.

9 Sell Like the Grateful Dead

Most rock groups used to have their beefy security men take young people's recording devices away from them at the door. No one could record anything because the musicians believed that if you could do that, you wouldn't buy as much from that group in the music store.

The Grateful Dead were different. They *encouraged* you to record. They set up areas for you to help make the recording process easier for you. They believed in a powerful sales secret: The more you give, the more you get.

Grateful Dead fans became all the more passionate because of this. They made their recordings and played them for people who had never heard Jerry Garcia play the guitar. They went to more and more concerts, and when the Dead released a new album, they turned out in droves to buy it. By *giving it away,* the band became a group of millionaires and one of the best-known and best-respected rock bands in the history of the world.

By giving it away.

You can do the same.

Rather than make your prospect merely imagine your product or your service, let the prospect experience it. *Give* them some of it! Get them *hooked* on it!

When I was in the advertising business, I stumbled across this idea of giving it away quickly. When my ad agency was trying to sell its services to a prospective client, and we were in a showdown with two other agencies, often the client would allow all three competing firms a long presentation.

The other agencies would work up elaborate dog-and-pony shows to show off their agencies. Not us.

We wanted to have the prospective client *experience* what it was like to *work* with us. So we made our presentations interactive, rather than just a show. I stood up and told the clients that we were not going to put on a show. I said, "We have left you documents and folders that tell you all you need to know about our work and our track record. We aren't going to duplicate it in this presentation. We want to use these two hours to work with you and show you how we might solve your advertising problems."

I would then pass around index cards and ask every member of the prospective client team to write down a current problem, one that was really bothering them about their advertising, and to do it quickly without a lot of thought.

I would collect all the cards and pull one out at random. After I read it out loud, my staff and I would jump up to the white board and write and draw solutions to the problem. The clients would then talk to us and even debate with us, but we got to know them. And they got to see how we worked. And a lot of the ideas we gave them were of great value to them. So even if they weren't going to hire us, we had given them something of value that we told them they were free to use. More than anything else, we gave them the experience of working with us. So they knew what to base their decision on. Many more times than not, we won the account. We got the sale. Because we gave more up front.

Think in terms of giving, not getting. When you are always thinking about "What else could I give them?" you will be gaining miles on your competitor.

Vacuum-cleaner salesmen in the old days used to go door to door with their product. They would go into a home and throw all kinds of horrific dirt on the floor. Then they would demonstrate the vacuum's power to clean it up. They were giving the buyer the experience ahead of time.

Look for more and more ways to *give* your prospects the experience of working with you.

When I sell seminars, the most success I have ever had has been from first coming by the prospect's office and giving a 20-minute version of my seminar inside a sales meeting. My prospects receive value from the 20 minutes, and they are no longer buying some unknown entity.

My consulting clients are the same way. I like to consult with them for a while (even if they don't realize I am) before they decide to hire me as a consultant.

When I sell personal growth CDs and tapes to sales staffs, I will often give some of them out first to allow my prospective buyers to experience them. I will tell the sales manager, "Pick out some key salespeople to experience these. Ask for their feedback, and watch to see if their selling performance doesn't increase. Base your decision on the power of the work. Don't base it on anything else."

Many times people I have worked with have told me not to do this.

"Don't give it away when you can sell it," they say. "When you give such good stuff away, there is no incentive for them to buy."

I don't agree. I think it's like the goose that laid golden eggs. If you give someone one of the eggs, what does it do? It makes them want the goose! They can *have* a golden egg or two, but they have to pay big for the goose.

The more ways you can *already begin serving* people who are considering buying from you, the better the chance you have of winning their business.

So, rather than asking yourself, "What can I say that will make them buy from me?" try asking yourself, "What can I give them that would be of value to them right now?"

You don't have to give away the store. Just the *experience* of the store.

People buy things they are already comfortable using. That's why book clubs and music clubs became so successful. "Join our club and get your first five CDs for a dollar!" they would say. I used to wonder, how do they make money doing that? Then, after I'd joined a club or two I figured it out. By getting you comfortable with the experience of getting your products through the mail from them. They want you to already experience a new way of buying your music so you can learn to enjoy the process.

The best car salespeople use their free time calling people who have already been in to look at cars.

"We've got some new ones in this week in the color you wanted and I'd love for you to test drive one, just to get the experience of it."

Other car salespeople would spend the same time standing around the lot and complaining about the advertising. Or complaining about management.

The amount of brain energy it takes to formulate and communicate a complaint about management is the same amount that it takes to formulate and communicate with a buyer over the phone. When buyers narrow their decision down to two or three prospects, it is almost always the one they had the most communication with that they will choose. They will say they "trust" that person more, but the truth is that they have already experienced working with that person and being served by that person.

If you have prospects you would really like to sell to, figure out ways to communicate with them more. And figure out ways to serve them before the sale. When you start serving and giving before the sale, the buyer already has a trusted experience to base his or her decision on.

Every other rock group in the world would stop you at the entry to the concert and pull your recorder out of your purse or out of your hands and yell at you for even thinking of stealing the group's music.

Not the Grateful Dead. The Grateful Dead wanted to give you their music any way you wanted it. And because of that, they succeeded in building a devoted and fanatical following that other bands could only envy. Their recordings continue to sell today. There's a lesson in that.

10 Slow Down and Be Complete

One of the greatest problems people in sales create for themselves is the problem of life-scatter. Paradoxically, they waste time by doing too much. They place such a high priority on a speedy reaction to anything that comes up, they never settle in to the really important stuff.

The important stuff is a long, slow and relaxed conversation with a prospective buyer ... a conversation that has no urgency to it at all. It is a conversation that feels as if it is happening for the pleasure that it gives both people. You yourself don't need to be anywhere else but here. In fact, you don't *want* to be anywhere else but here.

That's not how most of us sell. Most of us sell frantically in between all the interruptions. Cell phones keep screaming at us like children with bee stings. Migraine lights flash on the phone panel on the desk. People's heads pop in our doorway like puppets saying, "Gotta minute?" "Gotta minute?" "Gotta minute?" The mind doesn't know where to turn next. It's being pushed and pulled and probed and pinched and slapped and popped around all day. Poor mind. Poor beanbag. No wonder it wants to quit.

Slow down.

Learn to enter your selling conversation as you would a large warm bathtub of rainbow soapy water. And once you're in there, stay until you are relaxed and comfortable.

11 Pick a Spotter

Once I started experiencing the real joy of selling, I knew it was vital that I make a clear decision: I will be completely responsible for all my daily activities.

Most people never do that. They wait for outside forces to push them, and then they push back. Like caged animals, they live in a stimulus-response world.

If their numbers dip down below expectations, they wait for the company to respond to that. Maybe the response is as simple as a sales manager giving them an activity log to fill out.

But this is not a powerful position for you. It is an infantile position, designed to bring your parents back into your life so they can raise you right this time.

Don't allow this to happen to you.

You want independent power, not more rescuing. Don't put yourself in this position.

If you realize that you are not making enough cold calls each day, find a spotter. Choose someone else on the sales team to partner up with and make it fun. Don't wait for management to talk to you.

In weight training, a spotter is someone who stands over you while you are lifting weights. The first function of the spotter is to keep you safe. If the weight starts to fall, the spotter grabs it and helps you return it to the stand.

But even more important than that is the encouragement a spotter gives you. A good spotter will help you hold yourself accountable for your activities.

"Come on, baby, you can do it. Just three more! Don't quit now, push through it, two more! You're looking strong, one more, YES! YES!"

Even body builders like Arnold Schwarzenegger use a spotter.

"Come on, Arnold," says Arnold's spotter. "Five more, Arnold, roast them, Arnold, feel the burn, no pain no gain, yes! Beautiful, Arnold!"

You can do the same thing. If you realize that you are not making a sufficient number of pure prospecting calls to keep your harvest going, partner up with another member of your team. Tell that person how many contact conversations you are committed to each day, and what you want your total to be for the month. And offer to return the favor for your spotter.

Once the two of you are committed to it, it becomes fun. You hold each other accountable in ways that your inner voices might not be good at yet. Besides, you may have too many inner voices at the beginning of your sales career trying to talk you out of difficult activities.

Yes, it's true that this cold call you are now about to make will probably (if the law of averages is still in effect) not amount to anything. But that fact fools your brain into thinking that the call has a high potential for being a waste of time.

That thinking has to stop.

Think of it this way. If the worst hitter on a baseball team could double his trips to the plate each game (letting him bat first and sixth in the lineup) he would have more hits than the best hitter in the league.

The same is true in sales. Anyone on the team can double their trips to the plate. The more calls you engage in, the more *very interested* prospects you will find. Get the emotion out of the equation. Get the idea of rejection out of the equation. Have it be about statistics and the law (the *law*) of averages.

Partner up with a spotter and seize the day. Take complete control of your own activities. Don't wait for a rescue to take place. Jump out ahead of the statistical curve and let the universe take care of the rest.

12 Know How Desire Works

Wherever you are working in sales, there will come a time when you get some kind of technique-oriented sales training. You'll learn a sales system.

If you are still wavering on whether or not you want to be great at sales, that system, whatever it is, won't work for you. You can't put a system on top of a wavering desire and have it work.

You have to strengthen your desire first. You have to achieve maximum clarity on why you want the money.

Sales systems are only fun and useful once the passion and desire are at their maximum. That's when you'll listen to a system. Especially a system for selling. That's when you'll use it to the max. (Although you'll probably revise the system so many times to fit your own style that it won't be recognized by anyone when you're through.)

People aren't trying to deceive you in self-help books when they sell you a system that "worked" for them, but what they don't tell you is that it wasn't the system that got the result, it was their desire for the result. When the desire for a result is strong enough, almost any system will work.

Let's look at how desire gets what it wants.

Let's say I'm in the basement, hot and working and feeling thirsty.

First, I say "no" to this feeling of thirst. I don't want to be thirsty any more, I want that feeling to be quenched. That's step one. (Always know what you don't want … that gives you your *stand*.)

Then, I notice that I am picturing some orange juice. (I didn't have to force the picture into my subconscious mind, or from the left side of the brain into the right; the picture was already there, courtesy of my desire.) Step two is always a picture.

Picture the orange juice. I can see it now. I can touch it and taste it in my mind. That picture dominates my mind. So my body starts to stir. It pictures the route up the stairs to the cold orange juice in the refrigerator. Cold orange juice!

If something stops me or diverts my attention from the trip to the orange juice, it's not for long. If the dog runs up to me and I stop to remove a burr from his paw and I go down into my Yogi Berra crouch to pet the dog, I am no sooner in that crouch than I come right back up out if it. Why? The orange juice.

I have not lost my picture and soon the picture is pulling me toward it again. (We live into our pictures!)

Now I'm at the dark at the top of the stairs and now into the kitchen and at the refrigerator door. Now I've got the carton in my hand and I give it a swirling shake to give it the right composition and I'm ready to pour. I see that it's called "Donald Duck Orange Juice."

"Cold duck!" I say to myself. "Nothing like it when you're thirsty."

Then I pour myself a tall glass of orange juice and I drink it down just as I pictured I would.

And that is how people get what they want. That is how the brain manifests desire. All day long, we use this process to get what we want. All day long.

We automatically use this process for the little things in life. Why? Because it works. But we forget to use this process for the big things. Why? Because we don't have the same clarity and simplicity of desire for the big things. If we did, the same process would work, in the exact same way.

But, now, notice something different.

Notice what happens when I don't have any real desire for the orange juice.

I start upstairs for no real good reason, maybe just boredom, maybe I just think I should get something to drink so I don't get dehydrated, and the dog comes up and I remove the burr. Then, captivated by the charm of my dog, I might even follow him back outside and toss him the ball and then talk to the next-door neighbor over the fence. Next thing I know I've hopped in the neighbor's truck with him and I'm getting talked into trying to pull off a quick robbery at the convenience store and then end up doing five years in jail. Distraction upon distraction. The enemy of all achievement. All from not centering on my true desire.

Your best sales system will always be your clarity of desire. When you know exactly what you want and why you want it. That will do more for you than any technique in the world.

13 Live Person to Person

Enjoy the pleasure of living life person to person. There's a reason why society rewards you faster for success in this profession than in any other. You bring the people of the world together. Because of you, the poor people of China now know how to see money differently. You have taken an "evil" away. You have replaced it with the thrill of personal exchange.

In sales you are on a fast track to understanding people. What makes them tick. Doesn't that help you in your private life? Sales is *about* mastering the art of creating relationships. You are in an accelerated program for building self-confidence and inner strength in the face of your "people challenges." Nowhere else does it happen so quickly.

In sales you also master yourself. All the wonderful and new phases to your personality, grown and added to with each encounter. Most people freeze their personalities at the high-school level and keep them that way for life. Not you if you sell for a living. You just can't. You have to be like the plant that keeps blooming new flowers. You are never the same. You keep learning who you can be, and it changes for the better as you go along.

In sales you own your life. It is "You, Incorporated" going to work each day. Although you technically work "for" a company, when you're in sales, the whole company works for you. Even your sales manager works for you. So does the president. They all exist to see you succeed, and they will all help you succeed any way they can. Do you need them to help you with a big deal coming up? They will help you. I'm telling you, they all work for *you*! Who else has *that* in life?

14 Tuck That Puppy Under Your Arm and Go!

Pick a place you want to be with your customer. Then get into action in that direction. Don't consult your feelings. Don't consult your self-doubt.

Self-doubt is like a puppy you tuck under your arm before running across a six-lane highway. Previously, as you were walking the side road, that puppy might have been your whole mental focus. But not right now, because you have decided to make the run.

Most people (including me, most of my life) think they have to get rid of that puppy before even thinking about making the bold run. Given how this self-doubt preoccupies the mind with all its whining and squirming, they can't even imagine themselves making a bold run at something until it's gone.

But their only options will always be these: (1) Attend completely to the puppy all day long, or (2) Tuck that puppy under your arm and *go*!

15 Talk to Yourself

One of my biggest breakthroughs in the art of selling occurred when I discovered the power of talking out loud to myself. There is something really magical about talking out loud to an imaginary customer.

You will only know how powerful this seemingly silly practice is if you give it a fair try. I urge you to give it a fair try.

Here's how I now do this: If I have a big sales call to make today, I want to make sure that I am completely at ease talking to this targeted person. So I want to build a mental history, a conscious memory, of *already having had* a really great conversation with him.

I want to be sure of myself. I want to know that I know the best way to say these things. I don't want to fumble around when I meet the person. I want confidence. I want inner strength.

So I may begin my conversation in the shower. I may talk and talk as the water cascades around me. As I shave I may keep talking, making even better points and telling even better stories as I answer many imaginary tough questions.

In my car, it is even easier. Because of all the weird telephonic devices available today, it no longer looks crazy to be talking while driving alone. For all that next driver knows, I'm hooked up to some subtle internal earplug and dashboard mouthpiece. Who knows?

The fun part of it is that I am often about halfway through saying a lengthy, boring answer and I shout out, "Oh no, wait! Here's what I meant to tell you about! Your top competitor was involved in a very funny story last year…"

As I talk on and on I become even clearer and more "sold" on my own product knowledge. I keep finding better and better stories to tell. And I also discover more questions to ask and better ways to ask them.

The result is that when I am finally in the waiting room, waiting to see the Intimidator, I am not feeling blank and edgy and empty. I am feeling warm and well-prepared. I feel that gentle kind of anticipatory stage fright I feel right before a wonderful performance.

I can't stress how much more valuable it is to do this out loud. To truly talk it out. Most people in their cars either have faces full of worry and self-doubt, or they are listening to something annoying and appalling on the radio. Look around and notice these people while you drive. Look at those faces. Do you feel like they do? You don't have to. You could be engaged in a wonderful and witty conversation that's winning over your toughest customer.

When you keep fear and worry locked inside your head, it brings on migraines and more fear. It affects your stomach. Your whole nervous system gets edgy.

When you speak out, really step up and *speak out*, you are back in command of your own voice. Your own soul. It is a bold and provocative thing to do. (Your competitors don't do this. They are listening to the alarming news on the radio.) Speaking out while you drive makes you familiar and comfortable with the sound of your own voice. And it gives you experience.

"It's not really the will to win that's most important," Bobby Knight used to say. "It's the will to *prepare* to win."

16 Keep Your Eyes on the Prize

Always start at the end and work toward the beginning. Start in the future, and then come into the present.

With a new prospective client, know what you want to have happen at the end of the selling process. Begin with the ultimate outcome clearly in your mind. Then live backwards. To now.

Children intuitively know how to come from the outcome into the present moment. When someone is coming from the outcome, as a child does, objections don't seem that scary.

"I want ice cream."

My boy was five years old. I was not doing so well financially, and we were on a strict budget. I had been through tough times, and I carried no credit cards.

"We don't have ice cream," I said. "How about a bowl of your favorite cereal?"

"No. Ice cream."

Ice cream was the outcome Bobby had in mind. Bobby was "coming from" this outcome with every thought and communication.

The first objection, *we don't have any*, was simply bypassed.

I said, "Bobby, we don't *have* any ice cream."

"Bastin Robins! Let's go get ice cream, please, Dad?"

"No. I don't have money for that. I didn't go to the bank today so even if we went to Baskin Robbins, there is no money to give them for the ice cream."

"You promised," said Bobby.

"What?"

"You promised last week. You said if we were good and kept the house clean you would take us for ice cream. You promised."

I was puzzled. I had just told him that I had no money for ice cream. That even if I took him there, we wouldn't be able to pay for it. But he had set aside that seemingly final objection and just kept going.

"You said you would always keep your promises."

"What?"

"You said once that if you ever promised us anything, you would always keep your promise."

I sat down and thought about that.

Later in the evening, as we all piled into the car to go get ice cream (after a stop at the ATM), I wondered further. Why is it that when kids are really clear about what they want, they don't hear objections? They don't take objections seriously. They just stay in the conversation.

Somehow kids know that staying in the conversation is more important than any objection is. Somehow they know that if you really wanted to get them ice cream, you would find a way to do it. Do you see the connection to sales?

17 Change Your Thinking

If there is an element of selling that makes you uncomfortable, you will usually subconsciously try to avoid doing it. Human beings all do that.

But mastery of a process, like sales, requires us to be as conscious as we can about what we are doing. The greater the consciousness, the greater the mastery. We can't blindfold our way to the top. The more we think about mastering something, the faster we master it.

My client Jeremy was someone who once needed a blindfold removed to find his true potential, even though he was doing well by everyone else's standards. Jeremy was the top producer on his team of computer software salespeople. One night he called me at my home in a panic.

"I have a problem that I need to resolve now," he said. "I have a deep-seated fear that I cannot shake that has affected my sales capability for some time now. It is the fear of calling someone new and not saying the right things and therefore losing any possible business there."

"What are your thoughts, exactly, when it's time to call someone new?" I asked.

"I keep trying to tell myself that I have nothing to lose, but my mind keeps making me think that I am better off if I wait," Jeremy replied. "It is taking me out of the game, and I am actually getting upset about it. Affirmations don't work and neither does just telling myself to do it. I have tried nearly everything. I am looking for a creative solution. This is the only major fear left for me to tackle. If I tackle it I feel that I can really start excelling."

I tried to reframe his problem.

"Do you realize where your major fear comes from?" I asked.

"I don't know, that's just it, I would like to know," he said.

"Your major fear comes from thinking you have a major fear."

"You mean I'm not afraid, I just think I am?"

"Exactly right," I said. "Your thoughts are everything. They can trap you, or they can set you free."

"If my thoughts are everything," said Jeremy, "what do you recommend I do?"

"I recommend that you return to your freedom," I said.

"What do you mean?"

"Deep down you are free. You are free to think anything you want. You can think about ice cream right now or you can think of a thunderstorm, and I could go on forever about the things you are able to think about at any given time. You have the freedom to think anything you want, any time you want. You can think about major fear, or you can think about major opportunity. You are free. You have total freedom. Return to it."

18 Sell from the Spirit

Sales is the most challenging profession in the world. It grows courage and creativity faster than any other job. And it is one profession where your skills are immediately rewarded. You can build your fortune in sales as fast as you can build your skills. What other profession gives you that fast-track guarantee?

And the courage. That's so huge. You can't win without it. In sales you must grow courage like a muscle in your arm, like the strength in your legs.

Selling is no different from enthusiastic and courageous living. Like living, it's based on creating interactive relationships. Master the art of selling, and you've mastered the art of enthusiastic living. Everyone lives by selling something. You can't escape this adventure. This is your big chance to master life.

Jump into it!

Selling successfully is the same as living successfully, except that in selling you're keeping score, so it's more of a game. And there's a clear and fun way to win. There is no one in life, other than a professional athlete, who gets to win as often as a salesperson gets to win.

It's this spirit of the game that motivates the most productivity in sales. It's the high spirit of going for the big win. You know when you've captured this spirit and when you haven't.

That's because you soon realize that there are two ways to sell—(1) from the unconscious gut, or (2) from the highly conscious spirit. If you sell from the gut, you will feel butterflies all day. You will feel tightness in your throat, a constrictive pain pressing down on your chest and a knot in your stomach. That's selling from the gut. And that's how most people sell—from their gut-level fear of *not* selling.

Then there is another way. It's an attitude that happy and successful salespeople seem to find along the way. It's a way they eventually use to amass a huge personal fortune. That other way is selling *from the spirit*. That's when they're in the zone. That's when they are one with the universe. That's when there is no sense of time passing. Or, as an excited salesperson told me in the middle of a big negotiation, "It's like life is a dance and death is a joke."

Some of the better professional football players report that when they've got their best game going, they can no longer hear the crowd. They play in an eerie silence, and the ball and other players seem to be flowing in a ghostly slow motion. The game slows down and gets quiet, and inside of that quiet the players themselves seem to speed up. They make the greatest plays of their lives inside that zone of pure spirit.

When you connect to that spirit, the game of life slows down and you find your own greatness.

You will find from personal experience that when you're selling from the spirit, you're not "selling" at all. You're flying. And serving. And connecting. Like a tennis player who has defied gravity and just left the ground. You are soaring above the ground. Just as you always dreamed you could.

So whatever you do, don't quit. Keep selling. Keep talking. Keep communicating. Your communications will connect. Your work will all be worth it. You will be rewarded in ways you can't imagine if you simply don't quit.

19 Know Your Life's Purpose

I'm walking through the room full of seminar students. They are all salespeople from one company or another. I want them to see how important having a purposeful life is to sales success.

So I am passing out a piece of paper to each person. On the top of the paper are written the words, *"What do I intend to use my life for?"* The rest of the page is blank.

"Please read the question at the top of the page," I say to the room. "Then begin to write. Write whatever you want to answer that question. List all the things you can think of. Come off the top of your head. Fill both sides if you choose to. Basically write down what you intend to use the rest of your life for."

Some people begin writing right away. Their pens and pencils are moving quickly, scritching and scratching can be heard as words fly across the page.

Many people, though, are not writing at all. They are staring ahead, looking puzzled. Or else they are staring at the page. They are staring at the question. They don't get it. They don't get this question.

Finally one of them raises her hand.

"I don't get the question," she says.

"What don't you get?" I say.

"I mean, is this about a mission or something?" she says. "Does it mean we should have some kind of major personal mission right now?"

"Not really," I say. "It just means to write down what you intend to use your life for."

"Life is hard," she said in a weary voice. "Don't pretend it's not. Just because you're some kind of motivator, don't pretend it's not hard."

"I'm not pretending that," I said. "I'm just asking you to write down what you're going to use your life for."

"I think I have to wait to see what life does to me first," she said. "Then I'll decide what to do in response to that."

"I'm not talking about anything that's happening outside of you. I'm talking about the life that's inside you. That source of energy and awareness that is *in* you. I'm not talking about outside events or other people. I'm not asking you about them at all."

"But I see myself as a product of circumstances, don't you?"

"When I'm in the victim mindset, yes, I do. But that mindset is a choice based on a response to a feeling. It is not reality. When I take a deep breath and wake up a little bit, I can take ownership. I can realize that I own my life. I do own my life. It's a matter of being totally conscious of that fact. Because it's a fact, not an attitude or a feeling. It's not a belief, it's a certainty. Either I'm connected to that certainty or I'm not. My life is my life. By definition. Your life is your life."

Most of the victims in the room were staring at me and her during this exchange. Most of the owners were still writing away, now on the other side of the page, listing what they intended to do with their lives.

The victims' pages were still blank.

Just like their future.

And their future will remain blank.

Until *someone else* comes along and writes on it.

20 Obsess on Your Product

Do you remember deciding to get a good grade on a test in school? You never minded studying some subject you weren't interested in, if it meant getting that grade. You didn't really mind learning obscure facts about history or biology if it accomplished a larger goal.

In fact, once you let yourself get into it, something odd probably happened. You actually increased your interest in the subject and began to feel that you were surrounding the subject with your mind and mastering it.

You can do the same thing in sales. If you want to increase your confidence and sense of mastery, you might consider doing more study. The more you know, the more it will show when you talk about it. It will even affect your voice tones. We speak differently, with more grace and more ease, about things we know a lot about. Our prospects pick those vibrations up.

The more you study, the more interesting *you* will become, because people like people who are enthused about things.

Most people who are not reaching their goals in sales don't invest the time needed to discover true product advantages and know them deeply to be true. It's time to do that if you want to succeed in a big way. You can make it just like college or high school, and burn the midnight oil.

Learn. Absorb. Reflect. Enjoy.

Sales management doesn't always do the proper work to sell the sales staff on their own product's benefits. But if you are an ambitious salesperson, you won't wait for management to catch up to you. Most people who are failing at sales blame management. They blame management for not providing them with enough training, territory, information, leads, expense account, etc., etc. If you catch yourself blaming management, you'll want to re-adjust your energy inward. Focus on yourself.

Fear and call reluctance often manifest as shame of selling something that is not as good as advertised . . . but the catch is that the product usually *is* as good as advertised. Your product often has a number of hidden advantages to it that you can discover if you dig deeply enough. If you are armed with lots of evidence of product value, you no longer have to have selling and calling feel so much like self-promotion. You can make it be about pure and enthusiastic communication of benefits.

If I have to talk about me and my worth, I might get tongue-tied and lower my price.

If I can tell stories about how and why the *product* performs so well, and what the reasons and rationale are behind the *product's* success, I can talk all night. That's the zone salespeople get into and love. You know that zoned feeling, when it seems that life is a dance and death is a joke. Get there.

21 Transform Regret

Regret doesn't have to always be so negative. It doesn't have to get you down. In fact, it can be like a diving board. A diving board is neutral. If you just stand or sit on it, it can't do anything for you.

But if you *use* it, it can boost you into the sky.

Regret is like that. It can lift you up into the air where you want to be if you use it. Or it can just be something you sit on while losing your motivation.

In the center of one sales office I worked in, I was always hearing a certain person say, "If I had that to do over again, I would ..."

I was willing to bet that it was not just in the sales office, it was at that person's family gatherings, too.

"If I had just stayed with Jennifer in high school, none of this would have happened." (Again, this is how life itself imitates sales, again and again.)

Perhaps you yourself have thought about how you would do something if you had it to do over again.

Often this daydream is about high school, where our limited personalities were formed to shield us from imagined criticism, peer pressure and superstitions about the fatal power of other people's opinions. We look back at some aspect of high school ... how we were with the people we were attracted to ... how we were out on the playing field ... whether we volunteered to perform in front of the class ... how hard we applied ourselves to certain things we could have been great at.

Regret kicks in: *I could have been GREAT at that! I could have*

KNOCKED everybody's socks off, if only I had realized back then what I do now about concentrated focus applied to one thing.

We wish we had it to do over again.

We regret how halfheartedly we did everything.

What we don't see as we daydream about the past is that we are going to regret what we didn't do *today* and this week and this month if we don't snap out of it. In other words, one of the biggest reasons we didn't live up to who we really could have been in the past was that the past also had a past and that past was where we were spending most of our time, even in the past.

The past is seductive. It is an easy place to go drift for a while. Sometimes for a long, long while. Because it can't change or surprise you or betray you. It is dead. Living in the past is like flirting with a corpse. You will never get rejected.

But once you snap out of it, regret can be good. Regret can flip you into higher consciousness, like a diving board, if you use it right. It takes practice. Like a diving board does.

Regret can be good as long as you immediately *convert* it into something you can *use* to gain power to create the future. Laurence of Arabia said that everyone dreams at night, but the truly powerful people in life "are the dreamers of the day." Because they *create* the circumstances of good fortune for themselves.

Learn to flip regret immediately. The minute you catch yourself saying, "If I had that to do over again ..." realize that you do have it to do over again. Right this minute.

If I realize I am drifting off into daydreams of missed opportunities ... maybe thinking I could have been a good basketball player as I watch March Madness on TV ... or thinking I could have been a good singer as I watch the Grammy Awards ... or a good actor as I watch the Oscars ... it's time to *use* that regret in that very moment and say to myself, *Do it now!*

Everyone on the planet knows that under the right circumstances they could have become great. They could have become truly masterful and admirable. A legend, even. Every single person on the planet knows this.

But then they waste this knowledge and certainty on regret! They say to themselves, "given the right opportunity I could have ..."

Put your greatness somewhere else. Don't keep putting it in the past. Put it into the present moment.

Is there any reason why this sales call you are about to make can't be the best conversation you have ever had with any human being?

One thing I can tell you for sure.

If it isn't even close, you will regret it.

22 Feel the Joy
and the Power

"You have to be taught to hate and fear
It has to be drummed in your dear little ear."
—*South Pacific*

The great adventure writer Robert Louis Stevenson said, "Everyone lives by selling something." But the sad truth is that only salespeople know that they live by selling something. Everyone else is unaware. Unless you count Stevenson.

A mother at home sells the rules of the house to her children. An accountant sells his reports and figures to his boss and clients. Religious leaders sell the attraction of the faith to their followers.

A teenager sells his father on the idea of a car.

When you know you live by selling something, you can really put life into your day. In fact, you can feel like you've put your whole life into a single day. First thing in the morning you can rise up smiling and getting ready to sell. You know you become masterful when you learn to enjoy the process. The whole process.

Selling makes the world go round. Other people say that "Love makes the world go round," but great salespeople know that it's the same thing. Pump enough love into your sales pitch and you will succeed.

As a salesperson you get to become a psychologist, a dramatic actor and a business entrepreneur all at once. All in the course of enjoying your day.

Yet, the overt power of the position of sales seems to threaten others. Because you are out there exchanging value for money, right up front with it, no apologies, you threaten others who are more covert in their work. People who hide out from life don't like people who are so up-front.

So you get movies like *Boiler Room* and *Glengarry Glen Ross* and plays like *Death of a Salesman* that attempt to denigrate the profession and make free enterprise itself look demeaning. (Ironically, most salespeople I know get a big kick out of these movies and plays and laugh at the caricatures in them. Most salespeople are not sensitive at all about what they do because they know it's what makes the world go round.)

Today you will see most of the popular culture demeaning the sales process and profession. You see most of society viewing corporations and business as evil. Sometimes, when taken to extremes, an entire society will try to wipe out enterprise and sales altogether. Socialist and communist countries that have tried this have found out the hard way that they were killing the human spirit in the process. They were killing ambition and the joy of living when they tried to kill sales. The Soviet Union's prison walls of no-free-enterprise came tumbling down after many years of trying to create a sales-free lifestyle for everyone. It killed the soul of the people. It stopped innovation and adventure. It led to tremendous poverty and addiction.

The human spirit was replaced by vodka on a rainy morning.

China, the largest nation in the world, is also waking up to free market participation. In a wild attempt to cure so many years of propaganda against financial freedom and personal achievement, China has now adopted a new slogan for its people: "Money is a good thing."

People in free countries have been singing that song since they were children.

China has finally realized what all American companies know: nothing happens without a sale. The sale is the basic human exchange of service and value. It creates civilization and progress. It's how we help each other out. I have something for you, and you have something for me. Civilization was built on the cooperation created by the process of exchanging value with each other. The salesperson is the ultimate knight of civilization's round table of cooperation.

Recently it occurred to politicians in America that we have two options when it comes to China: We can attack them and try to dominate them with force. Or we can sell things to them and buy things from them. Which would be more creative? Which would inspire the world?

Selling and buying inspire the world.

Many times people in sales will start to fall victim to our own society's demonization of the sales process. (For although historically, societies without business and marketing and sales have collapsed and ruined the lives of their people, here in America it is still fashionable in the media, in our schools, in much of our politics and in our popular culture to naively denigrate business, the free market, profit and sales.)

This cultural bias against business often makes a newcomer to sales more vulnerable to discouragement. Many times new people in sales will think, "I can't do this. I can't sell. I need to get out of sales."

When I am coaching people who feel this way, I try to help them relax about the whole subject. If they truly want to leave, I don't try to change them. But I do try to persuade them to stay on their jobs a little while longer just to learn the art of selling before they go. Because if they can learn to sell successfully, they can learn to do anything.

And, with sales skills, they will have guaranteed their job security for life. Even if we had 50 percent unemployment, there would always be a place for an effective salesperson.

Sales skills, because they are so bold and profound and powerful, can be used in any other profession to improve that profession.

So, while it's technically true that you can "get out" of your job in sales, you can't go anywhere where sales skills are not helpful to you. Even a singer, to reach greatness, learns to sell a song.

23 Quit Trying to Succeed

Today in a seminar I was giving, I placed a book on the table in front of me and then asked a salesperson named Dave to come up to the front of the room and "try to pick that book up off the table."

When Dave picked it up quite easily and looked at me like I was crazy, I said, "No. That's not what I asked you to do."

I then asked Julie to come up front.

"Now, thank you, please, Julie, *you* try to pick that book up."

Julie picked the book up.

"Sorry," I said. "Not what I requested."

Dave and Julie looked at me with expressions that said, "What do you mean?"

"I didn't ask you to pick the book up," I said.

"Yes, you did!"

"No. I asked you to *try* to pick the book up."

What I was illustrating to the group was that there is a huge difference between trying to do something and doing it. It's a huge difference. Like day and night.

If I tell myself that I am going to *try* to make some sales calls on the phone this morning before going to lunch, my brain hears it as a completely different communication than if I say *I am going to make four calls before lunch.*

In one case, the "trying" case, I am not using my mind to command my brain at all. I am simply stating a wish for a hoped-for effort in some direction.

In the other case, the one in which I specify the four calls I will make before lunch, I am using my mind to issue my brain a clear and crystal command. A simple but strong instruction. A quiet but irrevocable order.

Let's look again at what Dave and Julie did. I said "try to" pick up the book, but inside their minds they quickly changed the order. They translated it into something more actionable. Their mind said to their brain, "Pick the book up."

In order to not let me down or embarrass themselves in front of the room, they converted my wishy-washy "try" into "pick it up!" without being totally conscious of what they were doing.

It's so much better when we can do this *consciously*. Just as it helps me when I remember that "try" is a weak word that does not issue a command at all. In fact, the word "try" will suggest to my brain that this action might not get done. When I hear myself saying, "I'll try to finish that proposal by tomorrow," it helps to stop and take a deep breath and ask myself whether I really am committed to finishing that proposal by tomorrow. If I am, I'll change my wording (brain coding) to "will do it" by tomorrow. My mind encodes my brain.

What I often forget is that my brain is simply an impersonal body part designed to serve me. Just like my hand is. Just like my foot is. Just like my nose is. All designed to serve me. The brain all the more! The brain is designed to be the ultimate instrument of service to the mind.

And yet, when I underperform and slip in spirit, it's because that very gear has been stripped of the command function. I am not crystal in my communication from my mind to my brain. I am in my weakest mode, my *trying* mode.

If Nike had not overdone it in its advertising, the most powerful phrase to restore this command function in my biocomputer would be, *"Just do it!"*

When I say, "Call four people," it's the same as telling my hand, "Pick up that book." It is unlikely I would command, "Try to see if you can pick up that book."

The doorbell rings. When I get up to answer the door, it would never be in response to the mind-message, "Try to see if you can answer the door." (Not unless I've been shot and lie bleeding on the floor.)

But psychologically, when I repeatedly talk to myself about what I am *trying* to do and going to *try* to do, I *am* shot. I am on the floor with all my focus running out.

As you drive around today, think this over. Your mind tells your brain what to do. It can tell it cleanly and crisply, or it can offer up vague and weak suggestions. And the brain, because the brain is impersonal and only lives to serve, will carry the clearest commands out. If your mind tells your brain to do something, your brain immediately uses whatever body parts are necessary to get the job done.

If you're driving your car and your mind says, "Turn left up here," your brain responds by immediately activating the hands and arms, and a left turn is almost automatically made. That happens with anything you really, clearly want to do.

It can happen with your sales activities too.

But, if you communicate with your brain in "trying" terms, your results will be terrible. Or if you say, "See if you can get some calls in this morning," that message, too, is loaded with heavy double-meaning and pessimism. It is not a clear command at all. The brain knows that it can *try* without actually accomplishing anything. In fact, for people who are struggling with professional success, that's usually what's happening all day long.

"I am going to ask you to make ten sales calls every morning this week," my sales manager once told me when I was selling another speaker's seminars.

Why ten? I would ask myself. Why not just leave me alone and let me make as many as I can?

Finally I got the courage to ask him out loud.

"Why ten?" I said to him. "Why don't you trust me to try to do as many as I can?"

He said, "When we leave it to chance, it drops out of existence. When we track it, it finds reality. Sales go up. It's not babysitting. It's managing. See it any way you want, but I recommend seeing it as a contribution to your success."

I resented him.

But today I can see that he had the basic process right. Mind commands brain/brain commands body/body creates circumstance.

If I am thirsty for that glass of orange juice, I never say, "Try. Try to get some orange juice from the refrigerator. Just try. Make the effort. Make a decent show of it. Resemble someone who is trying to do it."

Instead I say, "Get the orange juice."

And because I do that, I always drink orange juice when I want to.

But in the important unresolved problem areas of my life?

I'm still trying.

24 Learn to Re-FOCUS!

A young salesperson approached me at a public seminar and looked down at his shoes before talking to me. I could tell he was embarrassed about something.

"I read one of your books last year when I was just starting in sales," he said. "It's what got me up to where I could finally make it financially. Now I'm coming to the end of my year and I'm finding it really hard to motivate myself to work. I only have a few weeks left and I'm really desperate for advice on how to get my act together."

I only had a few seconds to talk to him, so I chose a small piece of advice that has always seemed to work for me.

"Go for the longest walk in your life," I said, "and think of nothing but how you're going to end your sales year. Are you ready to make a decision to be extraordinary? If you're not, don't. Keep walking until you are."

I wanted him to be out walking because I believe in walking as a great way to focus our thoughts. If we are not out walking, we are always open to being distracted.

Try this yourself when you find your motivation going away. If you give yourself enough walking time with yourself, you will return home *highly* motivated.

When you are too distracted by too many things, your mind is scattered all around. You need a single focus of attention to succeed at anything. You can't be attending to a hundred different concerns. They will all grow worse.

It takes courage to succeed at anything. And it takes a huge gathering of attention to find the courage. Then it takes a clear decision that you won't go back on. At that point you simply turn it into a game. And then you play full-out.

And you will win big. And you'll use the way you won at this sales game throughout the rest of your life. It will teach you how to win at all other things as well.

25 Keep Sweetening
Your Network

You are practicing being a great salesperson every time you treat someone well. You are also changing the inner nature of the entire world.

If you go to the store and treat someone behind the counter especially well, they may treat the next person in line well and that person goes out to her car and treats her husband well, and...

... There is this person in a grocery store I used to go to who was a checker, and she always seemed so genuinely happy to see people. She was not artificially cheerful, she was the real thing. It always made me stop what I was feeling and reconsider my problems. I always emerged from that store a little lighter. Imagine how that affected the next person I met. Imagine how it then affected the next person *they* met. It probably went around the world a couple of times before it got back to the woman in the grocery store. But I know it got back to her. It had to. Probably someone gave her a great smile and even, on some days, a tip! (That was me.) Maybe she's the kind of person who says she's so happy in her work "because people are so great to me."

You have your own world. Your own network of clients, customers, vendors, professional colleagues, sales prospects, friends and family. Sales happen inside that world. Every time you treat someone—anyone!—in that world especially well, it alters the nature of that whole world.

This is a mathematical fact.

I was reflecting on the interconnectedness of the world one day when I got a surprising referral from someone I didn't even know was connected to the world of business.

"You treated me and my daughter so well at one of your public talks," she said. "You sent me a book as a gift, and you had no reason to believe I was anybody or could help you in any way."

After saying this, she gave me the phone number of her brother who headed up a large organization that I had been hoping to sell to for a long time.

"Call him," she said. "He knows who you are."

A lot of business came from that. There *are* no unimportant people. Every person is important.

Recently I decided that I had been spending too much time on my work and needed some time for myself. I thought it would be fun to get away from my sales processes altogether and curl up on the bed with one of those dark and fun Dean Koontz mysteries... something totally unrelated to my work. The more unrelated the better.

As I opened the book, I read the quote that Koontz had put on the first page, by H. R. White:

Each smallest act of kindness reverberates across great distances and spans of time, affecting lives unknown to the one whose generous spirit was the source of this good echo, because kindness is passed on and grows each time it's passed, until a simple courtesy becomes an act of selfless courage years later and far away.

26 See Yourself from the Outside In

Always put yourself in your prospect's mind. See yourself through your customer's eyes. Pretend you *are* your customer looking back at you. Do this as often and as much as you can.

It will show you the way to sell.

I want to use, as an example, something that *really* bugs me and has bugged me for years and years: The movie listings in the newspaper.

Why is it always so difficult to find out where the movies are in the paper? When I look at the front page of the paper and on the Index or Contents listing I never, ever see the word "Movies." So I have to go about my annoying search. Are they in the "Local" section? The "Lifestyle" section? The "Entertainment" section? The "Arts" section? The "Zeitgeist" section? The "Modernity's Post-Modern Flatland Boomer" section? The truth is, they could be in any one of those sections, or maybe none of those sections! They might be in "State" and "City"! This very morning the movies showed up in a section called "Today"! It's a new section that's only been running for a few weeks.

There is a reason why the paper makes it so infuriating to look for the movie listings. The paper thinks we know the paper. They think we know the sections of the paper through and through. The paper thinks we know what the "Today" section contains because, well, *they* know what the "Today" section contains. The paper thinks we are as fascinated with the paper as the people at the paper are. It is a case of astonishing self-centeredness.

The worst salespeople do the same thing. They assume that the customer knows all about their product and service and thinks about it all the time. Not true. The customer needs help remembering! Because the customer only knows *one thing* through and through and that's his or her own business.

27 Laugh Yourself into the Phone

If your sales work involves using the telephone a lot, you might want to try a trick I once used.

I used to come into the office dreading my phone-call prospecting activity. I would come in and stare at the phone like it was some kind of reptile. I would do anything not to get started.

I would even start *filing*! I would organize my desk, shine my shoes, fix the leg of the chair, water the plant, sharpen a pencil, copy some papers, dust the bookshelf, and call out to passers-by all kinds of inviting questions.

"Want to go over next week's presentation sometime?"

"Sure, when would you like to do that?"

"How about NOW?"

Then I learned my trick.

My trick was based on what happened when I was coaching someone else. A salesperson named Bob just couldn't get the calling process started. He could do it once he was doing it, but starting it was always a huge problem.

"Anything can be enjoyed," I said to Bob, "if you think long enough about how to enjoy it."

So I thought about Bob's cold calling. How might he enjoy starting it?

"Well, let's start here, Bob, when *do* you enjoy being on the telephone?"

After thinking awhile, Bob realized that he enjoyed being on the telephone when certain people were on the other end. That's what gave me my idea.

"When you go home tonight," I said to Bob, "Put all of your next day's phone prospects on index cards. Then, on top of the pile, make an index card for your best friend. Someone who works in another business not related to yours, but someone you always laugh with when you talk. After your friend's card, there will be two sales prospects' cards, and then there should be, say, your sister's card. She's always fun for you, right? Every fourth card thereafter would be somebody you love talking to, but you can't call them until their card comes up."

Bob lit up. He knew right away that he would look forward to this game. And, in fact, this game worked wonders for him. He couldn't wait to get to his calling each day. He would often put in cards for people he hadn't talked to for ages the night before. He really couldn't wait to get to them the next day.

The trick also helped to get Bob get each day started in a good mood. His first call always got him laughing and taking life a little less seriously. His calls to his prospects were then looser and happier than they otherwise would have been. He was in the right mood to chat.

Often the phone is like the water in the ocean. It isn't as cold once you get in it. It's first getting in that's hard. The same with cold calling. Many people report that they actually enjoy cold calling once they're into it for a while. The hard part is always getting started.

We humans are funny that way. We hate to get into the shower and then we hate to get out.

In sales, the fastest road to success is through thinking. Learn to think about all your processes from top to bottom. It isn't about forcing some happy "attitude" on yourself. It's about learning to outsmart yourself.

Don't "sell" like some uncomfortable businessman. Don't have that sad look on your face as you drive in to work. Put on an old Beatles album and get caught up in the humor, strength and joy of their music. Sing all the way to work. Or if the Beatles are too old for you, put on what makes you happy. Remember that it's a cold-blooded logical maneuver to get yourself into a really good mood prior to communicating with others. That kind of mood gives you greater energy and creativity and you succeed much faster.

Selling is best when it rocks like that. The selling profession doesn't have to be like some sad song. Or, if it is, then you know your assignment: It's to take a sad song.

And make it better.

28 Tell Me Another Story

Everyone loves a good story. Children are captivated by a good story. Even more than they are by television. Notice the difference in a child's eyes. When a child hears a good story the child is totally enchanted and engaged. If you say, "I'll tell you the rest tomorrow," they will say, "No, no, no!"

The great religious leaders of all faiths built their followings by the telling of stories. They didn't pass out videos or brochures. Great comedians always win over their audiences with stories. There is nothing like a story as a means for one person to win over another.

Stories sell.

Even in this age of videos and computer images and multicolored brochures, nothing can top a story told by a live human being. Nothing.

Yet many of the salespeople I work with have missed this point. Rather than telling a story, they make claims. They describe features and benefits. They talk price. They try to "sell" rather than enchant.

Let's say I am selling cars. And you have come in to inquire about my company's services and I am an ignorant salesperson who doesn't understand the power of stories to sell.

You: "I am interested in looking at the new Chevy Javelina. I hear they are good. Are they as good as I am hearing?"

Me: "Oh, yes. The Chevy Javelina has rear-bearing suspension, a V-6 engine and rack-and-pinion steering. And this week we have a special price of only $21,000. You will not regret buying this car."

You: "Uh huh."

Look at what has just happened. You are probably no closer to buying this car. When I launched into my product's features and benefits and made claims and assertions about it, I was only selling as far as you were concerned, and you were experiencing automatic sales resistance.

What is sales resistance? It is that internal tensing up and armoring we all do whenever we believe someone is trying to sell us something. It's how we put our guard up, and increase our consciousness to guard against falling for a rip-off.

There is more sales resistance today than ever before in the history of civilization. Why? Because we are in the excess-information age. From the moment we wake up we are receiving multitudinous sales messages. The morning radio and TV and newspaper are all filled with sales messages. Even our favorite morning websites call out with offers. As we drive to work we see sales messages on billboards and on the sides of trucks and buses, all while we're listening to them pouring out of the car radio at us.

So we have become more sales-resistant than ever before!

That's why it is a matter of survival to learn how to sell without selling. And one of the best ways to do that is by mastering the storytelling art. And by gathering an enormous repertoire of stories. And by practicing the telling of those stories all the time.

Let's look at the same encounter we posited above, but this time I am not an ignorant features-benefits-and-promises salesperson. This time I am a storyteller.

You: "I am interested in looking at the new Chevy Javelina. I hear that they are good. Are they as good as I am hearing?"

Me: "I don't know, but let me tell you about something that happened last week. There was a guy who came in here who was about your age. And he told me that he had been driving Fords all his life. In fact, he said his father and grandfather had brainwashed him to hate Chevrolets. They even had those classy and cute decals of a little boy urinating on the Chevy logo on the back windows of their family pickup. He said he felt odd even being here! Then I challenged him to spend fifteen minutes driving the Chevy. I said it might change his opinion forever, and he laughed and said it couldn't happen. Finally we placed a twenty-dollar bet on it. I bet him twenty bucks that if he drove the Chevy he would never buy Ford again. So he got behind the wheel and I got in next to him. He was so nervous even being *seen* in a Chevy it was hilarious. So, then I see him impulsively reaching for his pack of cigarettes. He then laughs nervously and says he realizes that there is no smoking allowed on a test drive. I said to him, 'Not true! You can smoke. Because the odds are that you will be the owner of this car soon anyway, so who am I to tell you you can't smoke in your own car?' Well, anyway, he drives for five minutes and all of a sudden he starts laughing. I mean, this guy can't stop laughing. So I ask him what's so funny. And he says he is imagining the looks on the faces of all his relatives at the family picnic when he shows up in this car. And I say, 'So you understand this car?' And he says, 'You just won twenty bucks.' Well that's not even the half of it! A week later his father and grandfather rolled in to buy their own Chevy Javelinas. I noticed, too, that the little urinater had been scraped off of their rear window."

The beauty of a story is that it bypasses sales resistance. A good story will light up the imagination of the buyer. A good story will require that the buyer picture things. It will connect with that eager wide-eyed child in every buyer.

When you hear a question like, "Is this really that good?" please don't answer with claims, promises, features and benefits. Answer like this:

"A woman came in yesterday, she had a dog under one arm and ..." and relate an interesting human story about how your product has worked for someone else.

29 Ask More Innocent Questions

If you are like me, you have taken a lot of sales training classes and seminars wherein you have learned all those question-asking "techniques" for closing the sale or "qualifying" the prospect.

I hate those questions. Especially when I'm on the receiving end.

First the questioner "establishes bonding" by asking a totally insincere and offensive question such as, "How was your weekend?"

Do they really want to know? They don't even know who I am and they need to know how my weekend went?

Sometimes I like to cross up these phonies by saying, "How was my weekend? Bad. Terrible family picnic. Six dead, many more wounded."

"Excellent, sir, you're probably wondering why I am calling you?"

"No, I'm wondering why I picked up the phone, and why I'm still on."

"Oh, ha ha ha ha, sir. I think a sense of humor is really important, don't you?"

"No."

Whenever someone is trying to sell me something and I get a "qualifying" or "closing" question, I get even more annoyed.

"Is there any reason why you and I can't start doing business together right this very minute?" a salesperson will ask me.

"Yes. One I can think of . . . you. You are the reason. I won't do business with people who try to manipulate me with leading questions. I am not a child. You can't practice entrapment on me. Try it again, and I'll kill you with my bare hands."

"If I can get that price for you, are you willing to sign the papers today?" is another one.

"Why don't you just see what price you can get me and we'll talk afterward," I say. "Don't try to force a promise out of me."

Another trick taught in a lot of sales training classes is to ask, "When would you like me to meet with you, Wednesday afternoon or next Monday morning?"

"Wednesday or Monday? Where did those days come from? Did I have a blackout? Am I drinking again? Did we narrow it down to two possibilities already? Or do I just seem like a moron to you?" I want to ask. "Do you actually think I'll choose one of those dates because you tricked me by having them be my only choice?"

Sometimes I like to answer this way, "Neither of those times works for me, and do you know why? I did not tell you yet that I wanted to meet with you. In fact I was considering meeting with you until you used that cheap *alternate dates* trick which tells me that you do not see me as a human being but rather as some kind of stupid sales target. Why don't you go off your script when you talk to your next prospect? Why don't you throw your script away and just have a sincere conversation, person to person? I think you'll sell more."

I hate being boxed in. I hate being manipulated. It feels like entrapment. (Because it is.) I hate getting asked all those questions salespeople have learned in sales training courses. They don't work on me (or anyone else I know). They are about 40 years old. They worked 40 years ago, but we have all been flooded with sales calls since then so sales manipulation no longer works on us.

Make sure your questions to your prospects don't paint them into a corner. Most people don't like being interrogated or cross-examined. Especially by an unknown person.

Your role is not to force someone down a one-way rhetorical street. You are not living your life with a mission to set verbal animal traps all day. Your role is to gently open up a conversation with someone. You want to welcome someone into the conversation at their own chosen speed. You like to ask questions that reflect curiosity and a genuine desire to serve. Your questions are simple and innocent. They are courteous. You are respectful. You won't lose any opportunity that way.

You'll also know when it's time to "close." You'll know how to ask for the sale when the timing is right.

And I'm not recommending beating around the bush or "hint-hint" selling either. Sometimes the most profound and powerful closing question can be gentle and innocent as well.

"Do you feel like you're ready to make your decision right now?" is a good question, or, "Is there more you would like me to do to help you think about this offer?"

There is a core problem with techniques and scripts. They don't take into account how different people are. One person may be simply bored by clarifying questions, while the very next person you talk to may feel threatened by them. No technique in the world can "work" on everybody.

Open your next call by being gentle and inquisitive. Be like water. Be open, deep and clear. Listen quietly and your customer will sail right into your future.

30 Create Great Relationships

I believed that I had already written a pretty powerful book for salespeople awhile back when I wrote *50 Ways to Create Great Relationships*. But over its first months it had not found as big a business audience as I had predicted, despite the fact that most of the salespeople who read it liked it and saw it right away as a tool for building sales.

However, it is now clear to me that many people in the bookstores who bought it, bought it maybe hoping for something else. In fact, it seems that the title, having the word "relationships" in it, might have drawn a large number of "Oprah-viewers" who thought it was about love and heartache and betrayal. I even had a number of people tell me that they thought it was written as a follow-up to Paul Simon's "Fify Ways To Leave Your Lover."

And then, one day when I looked the book up on Amazon to see how it was doing, I noticed that Amazon had announced that "readers who bought *50 Ways to Create Great Relationships* by Steve Chandler also bought: *Succulent Wild Woman: Dancing with Your Wonder-Full Self*"! That just about sealed my regret for using the R-word in the title of an otherwise useful book.

So this book you hold in your hands has no such R-word in the title. But relationships are what selling is about. How you relate to people, and how they, in return, relate to you. That's what selling comes down to. The final conclusion is this: It's all in the relationship.

In one respect, when you sell your product, you are also selling yourself. Because, in the end, there is one ultimate thing that buyers want to know, and that's whether or not you are going to take good care of them. So, there's one primary thing you have to convince buyers of: *They will be taken care of.* At the end of the selling process, the final buyer's question is always, *Will you take good care of me?*

In this, your style, technique and personality mean nothing. Your obvious and demonstrative desire to serve your customer and go the extra mile mean everything. That customer cares not whether you are a fashionable charmer and an outgoing fraternity-boy super male towel-snapper of a bonding buddy. You could be a shy and homely introverted nerd. Whoever you are, you must convey only one convincing promise: *I will take good care of you.*

31 Use Your Reticular Activating System

Selling is about thinking. Selling is a chess game. Selling is like a mystery to be solved. Selling uses the brain.

Successful selling is *always* about using the brain. When you have an understanding of how your own brain is designed to serve you, you sell more.

One of the most fascinating aspects of the human brain's power is its reticular activating system. That's the tuning capacity of your brain. It tunes out what you don't need from the external world and tunes in what you need. It will find anything you want it to find for you.

How does it know what to find? It *doesn't* know until *you* tell it. The brain is impersonal. It waits for your mind to give it information. Whatever your mind dwells on, your brain will find for you in the environment.

Have you ever noticed that when you learn a new word, you start seeing it everywhere? How does that happen? You are reading a book or a magazine article and you see a word that you have never seen before. What does this word mean? You look it up. Ah, so that's what it means.

Then a strange thing happens. You start reading that word everywhere. Coincidence?

No! The word was always there. It was always everywhere. It's just that your tuning system, your reticular activating system, had been tuning it out. Now it tunes it in.

Notice what happens when you get a new car. You love that new car and you think it is beautiful and unique. But after a few days on the road, something odd happens. You start seeing the car everywhere. What's the deal? You thought you had a unique car. Now someone has gone and sold a hundred of them to a bunch of other people on the day you bought it? No. They were always out there. It's just that your reticular activating system had never tuned them in for you before.

If you are shopping for an apartment, you slow down and look at apartments everywhere you see them in the city. Then, even a few weeks after you have chosen an apartment, you keep slowing down to look at apartments. Your mind has made them important to the brain. It will take awhile for the brain to tune them back out.

As you walk through a crowded airport you hear hundreds of messages over the public address, over the TV monitors, from other passengers yelling into their cell phones, and you have tuned them all out so that you can think. You're having a nice little internal dialogue with yourself as you walk toward your gate when all of a sudden you hear your own name! It is asking you to please pick up the white courtesy phone. How did you hear your own name so clearly while tuning everything else out? It's simple. Your reticular activating system listens for your name. Because it encounters your name every day, on checks you write, on your e-mail, when people call you, etc. Your brain is highly attuned to it.

Whatever you think about for any duration of time will start to turn up in the world. It was always there before, it's just that your brain doesn't notice it until your system is activated.

By you.

If you haven't had a romantic relationship in a long time, you will probably be thinking more and more about it in your free time.

What happens then? You start seeing beautiful potential partners everywhere. It's very distracting! What you think about starts to show up.

The same is true with sales opportunities. If you spend time thinking about opportunities, you will start to notice more and more opportunities. If you think about problems, you will see more and more evidence for problems.

If you are a sales manager and you run your whole sales meeting focused on good opportunities in the market and good results from the past two weeks, your people will start to see opportunities everywhere.

My children used to play a game called "Bug!" when we were travelling in the car. Whoever saw a Volkswagen Beetle would yell out, "Bug!" and they would be ahead by one. Pretty soon our trips were punctuated by shouts of "Bug!" I found that even after the trip was over, and I then drove in to work the next morning, if I saw a Volkswagen I would mentally say to myself, "Bug!" It would often take weeks to have that reticular process fade away.

I sat in a sales meeting recently and the manager opened the meeting by telling everyone that he knew that times were tough.

"The local economy is not good," he said. "People are not spending money. They're scared. A lot of businesses are going under so everyone's holding their cards close to the vest. We're all going to have to work a lot harder than we're used to because of this."

He believed this was true. He believed that he was furthering his reputation with his team as a man of tough talk and no BS. He wanted everyone to see him as a rugged realist, not a rah-rah dreamer. He wanted to wake his salespeople up to what was really happening.

But what was he doing to their reticular activating systems?

He was programming them to find evidence for "tough all over."

When they left the sales meeting and passed a "Going Out of

Business" sign on the street, it was a sign they wouldn't have noticed before. But because of the negative sales meeting their brain's reticular activating system zeroed right in on it.

"Oh look, over there, there's another store in town going out of business!"

In truth it might have simply been a furniture store. It might have been their seventh annual going-out-of-business sale. But the meeting gave it a new grotesque visibility. Just as focusing on the bad always makes the world look grotesque.

The sales manager and I had a long conversation after that meeting, and his next week's meeting was decidedly different. He had saved a number of stories from the paper during the week about new businesses coming into town. He also gave a talk about how some of their big competitors, whom he still stayed in touch with, were now scared and laying people off and spreading self-fulfilling doom and gloom buzz throughout their organizations. He got excited and jumped up from his chair.

"Don't you see what an opportunity this is for us!" he shouted. "This is our time to move. Businesses are more open than ever to looking at new ways to save money. That's our competitive edge. The time is perfect to get aggressive and press our advantage. Let's go out there and help people build their businesses back up. Let's be there for them during these tough times so that when the economy breaks our way, we'll already have all the relationships we need to capitalize. As the newspaper stories I read to you prove, this economy is already beginning to turn. If we are there for people now, they will really be there for us later. Who do you remember most in life? Who do you cherish? Isn't it the people who come to your side when you are hurting? We'll let our competitors be seen as fair-weather friends. We will be the opposite. This market today may be the best sales opportunity we have ever had. Right now, we have greater chances of creating relationships than ever before. Let's go out and get to know our prospects. Let's be there for them. Let's listen to them. Hear their pain. Be there to help solve their problems. We'll own this town. *We'll own this town!*"

For the next two weeks the salespeople on that team reported back that they saw nothing but opportunities out in the community. They kept finding opportunity after opportunity to build lifelong business partnerships based on being there for people when times were tight. Sales began to happen.

Their version of "Bug!" was opportunity.

Whatever you talk about most in your mind is what you will find in the world. It's a scientific process in the brain called the reticular activating system.

Most people call the effects of this system "synchronicity" or "coincidence" or just plain "good luck." But the people who describe life that way, as a carnival of accidents, tend to be unnecessarily fearful. They tend to be victims. They don't feel like they are in charge.

They don't know how their brains work.

The more you learn about the amazing power of your brain, the more you will sell. Selling is not about circumstances and luck. It's about thinking. It's about strategy and smarts. It's a calculating and intellectually thrilling adventure.

Great things will start to happen when you get a deeper understanding of this.

Start using your brain instead of the lower emotions (fear of not selling, fear of financial ruin, fear of criticism at home) to capitalize on the opportunity that's out there.

32 Put Your Hand in the Hand

Beware of the electronic virtual universe. It can be truly unreal. It can fool you and make you feel like you're in control. It can make you think you are connecting when you are not.

Always remember to be real, not just virtual. You can't count on a virtual relationship for sales to happen. Your relationship has to be warm and personal.

Too many people become addicted to e-mail and fax and voice-mail. It seems easier. It seems like you are in more control. You don't have all those uncertain human emotions rising up like they do whenever someone is talking back to you or asking you questions. You don't have an untrustworthy human to talk to.

Going electronic feels like communication. It feels like progress.

But beware.

Because, in the end, when everything else is equal, people buy from the relationship they trust the most. The person they have been with in person. In person, you can hear all the subtleties in the human voice. In e-mail, you can't. In person, you can see into a person's eyes. You can see the eyes twinkle. You can see them widen with worry. You can see them glaze over if you're talking too much. If you are in someone's office, you can learn so much about the person by the pictures on the wall, by the funny objects on the desk, by everything. There are tones everywhere.

I was in a prospective client's office recently, and while I was there he took a call about his niece, who was having problems. When he got off the phone, he looked very depressed. I, hesitatingly, asked him if he was okay.

"Oh, yeah, well, it's my niece," he said. "She's such a great person, so smart. But she's involved with drinking again."

"I know what that's like," I said. "I had that problem myself for many years."

My prospect seemed to pick up.

He said, "That's right. I remember reading about your problem in one of your books. I want to give her that book! She loves to read, and it would be a great way to reach out to her."

"I'll send you the book tomorrow," I said. "And if she wishes, she can call me after she reads it. All I have to share is my own story, but sometimes that's all someone needs to be inspired to get some help. She needs to get help. She has a great opportunity in all of this."

"Opportunity?"

"Yes, the opportunity to grow her spirit and help other people. Addiction is bad, but if you recover from it, in some ironic way, it's good. It gives you an experience of using the spirit that a lot of people never get."

My prospect was totally lit up by now. I won't share the entire story of how things turned out with his niece, but they turned out very well. And that's not even the point here.

The point is that if I had not been there in person, if I had been conducting all my communications by e-mail and fax, I would not have tuned in to the personal side of my prospect's life.

He and I never would have had a chance to grow closer. To be humans together.

Sometimes I catch myself hiding behind being "professional." I want all my sales relationships to be above-board and controlled. I want to only talk about business. But that is not the route to greatness in sales. I have to keep reminding myself of that.

Greatness comes from a network of relationships built on giving and sharing. Great salespeople make friends. They are not afraid to live life in a friendly and interactive way. There is no chilly or stingy hiding out. There is no playing life close to the vest.

Trust is everything. A trusted friendship is stronger than discounted pricing every time. Friends buy from friends. The more distant you are, the stranger you become. If you have the basic people skills it takes to make a friend, you can succeed in sales.

Why is this not obvious and easy? Because of fear. We have secret fears we don't even know about. We have fears that date back to childhood that cause us to age-regress whenever we are in a potential sales situation. We need to rise above that. We can. We can outgrow those fears quite easily. That's one of the many joys of selling.

To reach huge success, we need to risk ourselves every day. We need to offer ourselves up in person to other people. And if they are too cold and "professional" to create a friendship with us, well, that's not our problem. That's their problem, because they have not outgrown their own fears. But with continued acts of kindness and friendship, we can help them take their fears away.

33 Mend Before You Send

As preferable as personal communications are, sometimes you really do have to work with electronic and virtual communications. Sometimes e-mail is the only way to communicate something, or, as is often the case, the most effective and efficient way.

The important thing to remember in this case is to brighten up your messages before you send them. Because you can't be there in person to give your sentences those warm and quirky nuances your voice tones can give them, you must have a policy of, "First, do no harm."

Before you send your e-mail off, remember to check it for tone. Is it happy? Is it a contribution to someone's day? Is it a pick-me-up?

If you are a masterful sales professional, you are a difference-maker. You add value to everyone you communicate with every way you can. In an e-mail (or voice-mail or fax) you have a very cold electronic system at play. It is up to you to warm it up.

Before you send your e-mail out, check it for warmth and good cheer.

Here is one I almost sent to a prospect:

Got your message on budget. What you're basically asking me to do is to cut my price down to half of what my other customers pay. Is there anything else I can do for you? Wash your car? Walk your dog?

I was glad that I paused for a moment before clicking the SEND button on my computer. After awhile I came back to the message and, after only a slight bit of editing, I was able to pump in some good cheer so that it would be a happy experience to receive it.

Got your message on budget. Thanks for getting back so quickly. I truly enjoy working with people committed to bottom-line results and cost-effective strategies. Let's get together on this so I can show you how I've made the numbers fit your objectives. I'm in your neighborhood Tuesday. How does 10:30 look to you? I'll bring wine and cheese. (I wish.)

On top of my computer I have a reminder taped up for me to see. It says, "Make someone happy."

This stems from my belief that happiness makes people succeed. That's why I try to make people happy. I know that the happier they are, the faster they will succeed.

Most people believe that the opposite of that is true. They believe that success makes you happy. It does not. It's the other way around. Happiness makes you successful. It makes you more creative and energetic. It builds relationships faster. It's a very efficient operating mode.

My little "Make Someone Happy" sign keeps me centered on my commitment to brighten people's days whenever I can and lighten their load. It causes me to pause before sending the vicious, scolding personal attacks I so love to type up when things aren't going my way.

34 Use Your Enthusiasm to Sell With

Enthusiasm is contagious. Enthusiasm sells.

Once when my children were small, I took them to a huge public park to play on a Saturday morning. We had gone there a few times before, so my kids knew what the park was like: lots of people, softball fields everywhere, a mass of activity. My daughter Stephanie was five years old at the time, and she asked me if she could make lemonade and set up a stand at the park to sell it. I said, sure, and she got busy making the lemonade and finding the card table in the garage. Her younger sister Margery helped her make the signs that said, "Lemonade, 20 Cents a Glass!"

They had seen this done before, so they knew the system. You set up a table on a hot day, you put out your sign, and you stand behind the table and sell lemonade and you make money.

It seemed to them that they had the right system for selling lemonade. But a sad thing began occurring once we got to the park and they were all set up to sell . . . no one was going over to their table. They had found a spot for their table in the far corner of the park under a tall and shady cottonwood tree, but no one was buying their lemonade. I was not far off, watching, but far enough away so that they couldn't see me, and if they had seen me they could have seen by my face that I felt sorry for them. They looked so tiny and vulnerable standing behind their table. Nobody was buying their lemonade. I didn't know what to do.

Soon my attention was distracted by my little boy Bobby, who was a year old and in need of some cleaning up. So I momentarily forgot about the girls and their failed enterprise of selling lemonade.

And that's when the noise started. I looked up quickly and heard it again. Other people started looking over toward the noise, too. It was impossible to ignore. From the far corner of the park there were two little girls' voices taking turns yelling at the top of their lungs a single, blood-curdling word, "*Lemonade!*" Again and again, the word came screaming across the park, "*Lemonade! LemoNADE! LemoNADE!*" First one little girl's voice, then the other, louder and louder . . . (There was something almost subhuman about it, as if the voices were coming from somewhere deeper than a little girl's body. It was bordering on a Stephen King scene.) People in the park stopped in their tracks. Even softball players stepped out of the batting box to see what the commotion was about. What kind of chaos would cause this outcry of noise?

And then something strange and wonderful happened. Two or three at a time, people started walking over to the table. Soon a line was formed, and the girls' shouting had stopped. I could see Stephanie and Margery serving as fast as they could and gathering in money and making change.

I stared in admiration. I realized that I had just seen something I was always going to remember. I realized that the universe was showing me a glimpse of how people access their spirit to get what they want.

It had startled me a little to hear those spirited voices when they yelled. In my own youth, I *never* would have raised my voice to that volume in a park full of grown-ups. I probably would have left the park that day finding fault with the *system* of selling lemonade. "The sign was too hard to read. The table was hidden in the corner. There must be a better *way*."

What I heard in my little daughters' voices was a discovery of the spirit. It was the word made flesh! In the beginning there was the word, *lemonade,* and in the end there was a line of real live flesh-and-blood customers for the lemonade.

Our lives seem to keep giving us one lesson to learn: when you find the voice of your spirit, you can sell *anything.*

35 Cure Your Intention Deficit Disorder

Sometimes I perform poorly. In love, in parenting, in sales, in sports, sometimes I perform very badly indeed. But it is comforting to know that I can do something about it, and that the something I can do is always found in the same place.

My poor performance, in any area of life, comes from a deficit of intention: If don't want an outcome intensely enough, I will lose focus. The internal power has leaked out. Without enough power in the hose, you can't point the water, so you can't water the plant.

Lack of focus is why I don't succeed.

Every time.

Think back on the surveys that show that the average salesperson spends 1.5 hours a day selling. That's one-and-a-half hours a day! This is not due to laziness, either, because salespeople, whatever they are, are not lazy. It is due to a lack of prioritized intention. The *only one-and-a-half hours of selling* is due to not creating a purposeful day. We're not creating, we're reacting.

When a salesperson learns to control and guide his or her intention throughout the day toward nothing (*nothing!*) but the creation of sales relationships, then the deficit of purpose disappears and sales increase exponentially.

And there is a difference between "wanting it" and being "interested in having it." That very difference is the difference between my failure and success in all walks of life.

When two professional sports teams are going down to the final minutes of the championship game, you will often hear the announcers say, "This game is going to go to the team that wants it more."

"That's right," chimes in the color commentator, "it's a matter of sheer *will* right now. You're about to see the team that wants it most *will* themselves to victory. Always happens."

The salesperson who does not sell a lot almost always has less of a connection to his or her deep-down desire to succeed. The deficit in desire shows up as lack of preparation, lack of courage in the face of challenge, and simple lack of energy for the tedious parts of the job.

Ruben is a friend of mine who manages a large sales team. Recently, after he conducted a series of job interviews for an open sales position, I heard him say something like, "It's down to two people, and they seem pretty evenly matched in skills and résumés, so I'm going to pick Kimberly."

"Why her?" I asked him. "You seem pretty definite about her for having two people who are so evenly matched."

"On skills and qualifications it's a coin-toss," he said. "But, actually, it's easy for me. Kimberly wants the job more. You can feel it in the way she speaks, and you can read it in her follow-up letters and cards. Yesterday she made me an offer to come in and do a trial week to show me what she could do, no strings attached, no pay necessary! Someone who wants it that bad is someone I want here."

Whoever wants it more. That's who will get it. The stronger the intention, the greater the result.

We often think the *system* we are using to get something is not right. But we are wrong. What is not right is the *intention* we are using. What is missing is the desire to get that thing done. We buy books about systems all the time, not realizing that it's not "how to" that's important, it's "want to." The "system" is the great false promise of 99.999 percent of all self-help books. "How to" get what we want. The "how to" is not what's missing. What's missing is the "want to." The ultimate "how to" is *to want it more than we ever did before.*

That's the ultimate system.

36 Don't Solve Your Problems

In professional life, time is money. So anything we can do to eliminate time-wasters is a good move.

The biggest time-wasters of all are problem-fighting and fire-fighting. All those urgent little things that eat up all our time and keep us away from the really important things we know would move our business forward.

A serious casualty of fire-fighting is planning. There is no time for it. We don't plan because planning doesn't feel like problem-solving. It feels like we are ignoring our problems.

This is how we become addicted to problem-solving. We are so habituated to working on our problems that planning feels like a waste and a luxury. Planning feels like something we need to do sometime later when we don't have so many problems pressing in on us. Maybe at some retreat.

That's why people who master a version of the 80/20 principle of time-management (80% of your results come from 20% of your time) are able to enter a new dimension of problem-solving, in which problem-solving itself is eliminated from your day and replaced by "Producing What You Want."

Managers and sales professionals soon learn that being creative and productive can be an all-day-long operating policy.

Therefore their daily activities are designed not to make the problem go away, but rather to *bring what's desired into existence.*

Good professionals are more efficient when they are builders and producers and not reactive exterminators.

Therefore, their orientation to problem-solving is completely different. They don't focus on the problem. Once they clearly and accurately identify the problem, they watch it shrink down (to near-irrelevance) by placing it into the context of their Desired Goal. By focusing on what is desired instead of what is not desired, they expand their thinking above and beyond the problem and produce a solution, often so creative and imaginative that it's almost completely unrelated to the original "problem."

They see "problems" the same way a good quarterback sees defenses. It's just what's lined up against him. It's just the way the obstacles are lined up. Given that he sees how they are lined up, he will then *create* and *produce* a play designed to score points. The focus is on the activity that leads to scoring, not the obstacle.

You build your play around their defense. You move above and beyond it. You leave it flat-footed in your wake. And you can do the same thing with your problems.

The trick is to not focus on the problem itself.

Because when you focus on the problem, you do not expand your thinking, you reduce it. You narrow yourself down to the parameters of the problem. The problem takes on all the power. It defines the restrictions of your thought. That's why it is no fun to solve problems this way.

Great producers take a builder's approach. They are more like home-builders than demolition workers. They don't try to take something bad away. They try to bring something good into existence. They focus on what they want, not what they don't want.

Example: Martin Luther King was extremely effective in leading the civil rights movement in America because he didn't try to solve the problem of racism.

He was a creator, not a reactor.

He was a builder of solutions, not an extinguisher of bad things. He focused on his desired outcome, not on the problem. Focusing on the problem would have made him small and angry and narrow-minded. It would have made him destructive rather than creative. It would have turned him into a petty version of Malcolm X. Instead, he pointed everyone toward the goal. He called it his "dream." He said, "I have a dream." And then he said what he wanted, he described what he desired, a land in which black and white would be free to go to the same restaurants together, to attend school together and to live together in peace and harmony. So he set about to produce his dream. To produce his dream, he did not need to eliminate anything. He didn't need to exterminate or extinguish racism. He didn't try to get rid of racism. He left racism alone and created what he wanted. He expanded his thinking above and beyond the problem.

Racism was left in his dust.

Here's a more personal example of why problem-solving just causes more problems. Many years ago a friend of mine was newly divorced and lonely at night. She got so lonely she began to think of her loneliness as a "problem." So, being like most people, she set out to solve her problem. (But people who spend all their lives solving their problems are missing the whole point of the human brain. The brain can do so much better than that. It is not a born problem-solver and fire-fighter, it is a born creator, a builder of desired things, not an exterminator of undesired things.)

So, anyway. My lonely divorced friend thought she had better solve her problem of loneliness, so she went out in the evenings to the neighborhood bar to be with people. She met a man who was equally lonely, and soon they had a relationship going. But a new problem soon arose. (And that's the problem with problem-solving: problems are always replaced with new problems. Why? Because you still didn't build, produce or create what you wanted. If you simply eliminate a problem without creating a new structure to get what you want, a vacuum is formed, and another problem rushes in to fill the vacuum created by the originally extinguished problem.)

Now her problem was that she was in a relationship with a man who drank too much, was lonely and depressed, and wanted to hang out in neighborhood bars all night. Sometimes he got in fights. And soon the relationship itself was something of a problem, a problem she needed to solve. Given that this alcoholic lover of hers was also very possessive and jealous, it would become more of a problem than she imagined.

What has happened here? Where did she go wrong? Maybe if she had not jumped right into problem-solving, she might have had a great life by now. If, instead of asking, "How do I solve the problem of loneliness?" she had asked, "What do I want? What would I like to bring into existence?" she might have realized that she wanted to create a great relationship with someone she liked and admired. Focusing with clarity on that desired outcome would have moved her in a completely different direction. She would even have been willing to endure some loneliness while she continued her strategic search for the right person. She wouldn't have minded that because she would have known that she was on the right path.

This is why, once you have become a wise and creative professional, it is no longer appropriate and effective to spend your day putting out fires and problem-solving. You can focus on what you want, not what you don't want.

Let your problems be a signal to you that it's time to bring something new into existence. Something that will not only make this problem go away, but prevent others like it from continuously popping up.

37 Act As If

Figure out who *you* want to be in your professional sales relationships...maybe you'll want that person to be giving, creative, thoughtful, entertaining, warm, compassionate and intelligent with an eye toward extraordinary service. Once you have that Way of Being personalized, act as if (*as if*) you were that person at all times. It's a powerful practice, when it's practiced.

When a client calls, act *as if* that person makes you happy and you also enjoy making them happy. Act as if they are the most important person in the world to you. Act as if. Don't wait until they become really important, because then you are in for a long wait. By acting as if they are important, you have made them important. You have also joined the great dance and the great musical show of life...you are up on stage acting *as if*, while everyone else is waiting for "true feelings" to guide them.

Acting *as if* gives you access to your spirit. You bypass the contradictory emotions. You even bypass your own fatigue. The paradox is that enough acting *as if* leads to the real thing. Soon you are not acting any more, you are just *being* natural, in a happy zone, and success in business comes very easily to you.

My young friend said, "I wish I could get more interested in my English class. But it bores me."

I said to him, "Try this. Act as if it were interesting to you. Be like an actor. Act as if it were fascinating. Like you were in a movie with Britney Spears, and your part called on you to play a guy who was interested in the material. Try that for a day or two and see what happens. What do you have to lose?"

Two days later he was very happy because he said he was having fun in English. He was acting as if English were really important to him, and it was suddenly becoming interesting. "Creepy!" he said with a smile.

38 Find the Answer
in Your Hands

Whenever I went through a stretch of poor selling, I realized, looking back, that I was not being honest with myself about how much power I really had to overcome things. I kept telling myself I was helpless in the face of circumstances. But that simply wasn't the truth.

I had to ask myself: How would I make a daily policy of living in truth and enjoying the beauty of being alive? The answer was simpler than it looked. I didn't need a brain transplant, or a new injection of character or a change of DNA. I didn't even need five years of therapy.

A clue to the answer was found inside the purpose of the "powerless" lie. As I observed these "I am powerless" thoughts I was thinking to myself, I could see that they were all (each one of them!) designed to keep me out of action. They were all "call in sick" cards on the great game board of life. They made it easy to fall victim to my feelings (especially the negative ones). The powerless thoughts gave me cover for following those feelings (even though following a negative feeling usually leads to an even more negative one).

Therefore, if each of these powerless thoughts leads to passivity, then the answer must be found in activity. It is as simple as the saying your grandmother used to repeat to you whenever you helped her with a chore, "Busy hands are happy hands."

Our bodies and minds were designed for movement. They were

not designed for an agonized, depressing paralysis. Yet our current culture and society urges us further and further into the soft, lewd arms of comfort. Dark and clammy passivity beckons, and the world becomes obese with self-nurturing. Listen long enough to the lies and we won't move at all. We will just become shimmering mounds of glistening gel, wobbling discreetly in reaction to the latest electronic thrill, the shift of the cushions on the couch or the blast of the super-sized drink we slurp to wash down another sweet and spicy artificial food. We will shimmer. And we will grow sad. And we will tell ourselves more lies.

Your own way out of this cycle will show up for you once you base your life on constructive action. *What needs to be done?* That's the question. Not, "How do I feel about doing this?" Every time you ask yourself, "How do I feel about doing this?" or, "Am I comfortable doing this?" or, "Do I have the self-confidence to do this?" or, "How do I remove my fear of doing this?" you are robbing your soul of its greatest gift, the human spirit. You are placing emotion above motion. A near-fatal misjudgment. Emotion is meant to be carried low, and motion high. Lift yourself up, please! The human spirit is expressed in uplifting motion. A bird must *move* before it can fly. And so must we. Take these broken wings and learn again.

The late and great American philosopher William James said, "Effort is the measure of a man." And Japanese psychologist Shoma Morita said, "Effort is good fortune."

Today there were many people who did not go out running. Why? Because they didn't feel like it. But even the most devout daily runners, the ones you saw out running this morning on your way to work, *didn't feel like it.* Not until they started running. Then, about 15 minutes into the run, they felt like it. In our society we have everything backwards. We are all sitting around passively waiting until we *feel like* doing what we know needs to be done. We have now elevated feelings to the highest possible level. We've put them above everything else, and in so doing, we have paralyzed our lives. We have frozen perfectly good lives that could have been constructive and full of joyful accomplishments.

If we would learn to honor movement over passivity, we would have the answer.

The truth is, we *are* powerful. But we can only know the truth of our power by using it. We can't just know it conceptually, because that does us no good. We can't really know anything by just sitting there trying to figure out what we feel like doing. (We knew we were powerful when we were children, because we spent the day running, skipping, jumping, painting, laughing, singing, and soaring through space. Our young minds moved, too: creating, inventing, improvising and making stuff up all day long.)

As adults we have talked ourselves into a conspiracy of frozen living. The powerless thoughts we think justify the deep freeze we are in, the paralyzed existence. The weak, negative thoughts justify and explain why we are always so *stuck.*

Busy hands. That's the answer, and always has been the answer. You'll find your joy, not by believing, but by *experiencing* that your grandmother was right. Busy hands are happy hands.

39 Let Your "Weakness" Sell for You

A shift in perception can change a salesperson's life.

A good place to begin is with your weaknesses as a person and as a business representative. Because I am now convinced that you can *always* convert weakness into strength.

Learning how to use your "defects" in salesmanship can be your most exciting discovery yet. You start by relaxing. Try to learn how to relax into who you really are (comfortable with being) instead of who you think you "should be."

Laurie was my client and she was miserable. The other women on her sales team were what she called "sorority sisters." They all dressed sharp and looked sharp and had bubbly personalities and go-go energy levels. They talked fast and they finished people's sentences for them. Laurie couldn't stand that.

"I don't belong in sales," she concluded as we met to talk about another disappointing month she had had. I wanted her to step outside of her own anxiety for a while and look at her options.

"Sales is life," I suggested. "You belong in life, don't you?"

"Sometimes I wonder," she said.

"Well, then, let's not talk about sales for a while. Let's talk about you. Tell me about what you did before you came into sales. And try to remember, if you can, when you felt really happy while you were working."

"I was a waitress," she said, "if you can even count that as a job. It was hard. At least for a long time it was hard. And then I found this really great club, this really great restaurant, and after a few months there, I began to totally love my work. I got so good at my job that I looked forward to my customers coming in. The more the better. I began to love the challenges. And I was serving people really well. I had complete confidence in myself. I knew I was good. They knew I was good. And I got the most tips of anyone there. I just loved serving."

I could tell by her body language that her whole being was remembering how wonderful she used to feel doing that job. She took on a relaxed, softer mood. Even her skin looked warmer. Her eyes were softer and brighter at the same time.

"I got more tips than I ever dreamed possible," she said.

"No wonder," I said. "It's obvious that you were in love with your work."

"I was," she said. "But I can't go back and do that. I mean, I could, but in some ways I like this better. Or at least it feels more appropriate, selling, being more professional, being more of an executive than a day laborer. It's just that I hate it that I don't fit in. I'm not a multitasker. I hate using my cell phone in traffic and I'm not the sorority type."

"You're a waitress at heart, maybe," I said.

"Well, yeah, but what does *that* say about me? I don't want to go back to waitressing. That would be a step back. I might as well become a hippie or get some tattoos and try to gain weight . . ."

"Hold on," I said. "I said a waitress at heart. You can be a waitress at heart and succeed at selling too. If you want to succeed at selling, you can. Sales is life."

"Tell me what you mean," she said.

"Why don't you try something unusual," I said. "Why don't you take yourself back to when you were happy being a waitress. Who were you? Who was that person? Why don't you come to work tomorrow as her? Why don't you try to see your job here as an advanced position in waitressing."

"Can I wear an apron to work?" she said.

"In your mind, yes! When you cold-call on the phone, see that cold-calling as offering a menu to someone. You're not being pushy or invading anyone's space or privacy, you are *serving* by making an offering. Reframe everything you do. Give it a new explanation to yourself. See it *all* as service. Every bit of it. Stop selling and do nothing but serve. Stop selling. Be happy to serve people anything they want. Let them decide. You don't have to be pushy or hyperactive or giggle like a sorority speed freak with a valley-girl accent. Just be you. You, you, you. Be in love with you. The real and true you. The you who loves to serve."

"Wow, I'm liking this," she said. "But what about closing? What about all those tough, manipulative, grown-up, *manly* negotiating skills I have to use?"

"Did you do that when you were a waitress?" I asked.

"No. I just let them decide. When they hesitated or couldn't make up their minds, I made recommendations. I asked questions, learned about their tastes, and then I made recommendations."

"Then do that now," I said. "Ask questions. Learn about their tastes. Find out about their lives and hopes and dreams. Make suggestions when it feels right. But only when it feels right. Only when it feels like a service to someone having a hard time making up their mind. Serve all day. Take orders. And bring them what they want. Bring them the service they need to give them peace of mind. Peace of mind is a huge service."

"I am really liking this idea," Laurie said.

"And one other thing…memorize your menu! Know your menu inside out. Don't play dumb or confused or disorganized. That's an act. That's a covert cry for help. Learn your menu so deeply that it is a joy to talk about. All the dishes. How they're prepared. And . . . especially? Especially what sets the offering apart from what they get at other places. People want to know. And they want to hear it in your voice. Use the friendliest voice tones you can find. Tune up like a singer. A singing waitress. Don't go to your grave with your music still in you."

"Wow, that's beautiful," she said. "Did you just make that up?"

"Yes," I said. "It's a quote I made up by Oliver Wendell Holmes. *Most people go to their graves with their music still in them.*"

"Not me."

"Not you."

Laurie went on to have her best sales month of the year following that conversation. And Laurie is not an isolated case. I am just like Laurie. I don't feel like a "normal" salesperson. And you might be like her too.

When you find your talent for selling, it will become a socratic drawing out of the talent that's already there, instead of the old idea of "putting in" a system that was alien to you. Stop fixing yourself. Stop improving yourself. Stop trying to identify what's wrong. There's nothing wrong.

40 Stop Living off the Mother of Invention

Necessity is the mother of invention. You've heard that a million times. That's why salespeople do better at the end of the month than at the beginning. At the end of the month—because they think they need to—they invent ways to sell.

It seems necessary.

They see it as a real pressing need.

Has it ever happened to you? You lose your focus for the first half of the month, then crush, crush, crush, crush, crush comes the outside world. Crush come the spouse's questions. Questions and more questions. "When will we be able to ...? Why can't we? Do you have any idea if we can afford to ...?"

You're thinking, *Let me out of here. I never signed up for this. This was supposed to be a partnership, not an interrogation. Did I marry Dennis Franz?*

This kind of end-of-month necessity is not the ideal sales motivator. I know what you're thinking, you like to live your life like a wild animal, like a wolverine backed into a corner with only one option: kill or be killed. But I want to convince you that it's a bad habit. It's immature. It's ineffective.

Not only that, but you'll lose the light touch, the creative idea, the brilliant presentation, the huge contract. Instead, you scrap and scrape and then you *settle*. You settle for what you can get. It's the end of the month. You have to.

The best time to communicate with your most challenging prospect is *not* when you need the sale. Prospects would rather not talk to people who need, need, *need* something from them. Would they? Would you?

"I need you."

Would you leave that message on a prospect's voice-mail?

Let's lose that habit. Let's realize this: The best time to communicate with your most challenging prospect is right after you have made a sale to someone else. The second you finish closing the sale you should be in *immediate* conversation with the toughest cookie on your list. Because that's the "you" they will buy from. The happy, excited, self-confident you. And what's great, so great about who you are in that moment is that you don't need them.

They like you for that.

41 Why Not Take All of You?

When you go to work tomorrow, why not take all of you along? Most people just take the professional part of them to work, which is to say the narrowest and least imaginative part.

Try this: Make a list, either mentally or on paper, of what your best friends and closest family members like the most about you.

Let's say you had just died. And everyone was at your funeral. If it were your funeral, and they all got up one at a time, what would they say? What are the good things?

Do you have a hard time thinking of your funeral? Try it. The more you try it, the more alive you will become. Life needs death. No one is guaranteed tomorrow. Come on. Let yourself picture the whole thing. Picture what everyone says about you.

Okay, now that you have all the good things about you. Your humor. Your caring. Your love of dogs. Your love of movies. Whatever they would say, and you would modestly agree with.

Now take those things to work.

Put your best qualities into your job. Don't wait for some future perfect job, because there is no such thing (actually there is, but it's not in the future, it's in this fresh moment). Your job will be as perfect for you as you make it. Shape your job. Define your job with your own loves and desires.

Pour yourself in as you would water into a potted plant.

If you are a good and witty and thoughtful note-writer, take a deep breath and write one of those notes to your most important customer. If you love movies, find the customers on your list who also love movies and call them once in awhile to share reviews.

Make your job conform its shape to you, not the other way around. Find subtle ways to work yourself in.

One of my favorite clients, Tom, loves Bob Dylan and poetry and movies. We always enjoy e-mails and phone calls and lunches on those subjects as we also mix in a little business here and there.

The transition is easy because we have become friends. I sell to him naturally and easily. He buys from me with pleasure. When the costs don't work for him, we have no problem being open and honest. Why wait until work is over to have fun?

If you are good at something (which means, *if there's something you love doing*), work it into your job. Any way you can.

My good friend Crystie is an office furniture salesperson. After we first got to know each other, I found out that her passion was photography.

"Why not take your camera with you when you drive around your territory calling on businesses?" I suggested. "Just always have it in your car. Maybe some days you'll be inspired to take a wonderful photo of your customer's new office building. Frame it and give it to him on your next call. Set yourself apart from the competition. Be who you are. Integrate your loves and passions into your work."

She loved the idea. She jumped on it.

Don't be afraid to be different from your mental picture of the "normal" salesperson.

For five years of my life, I wrote songs and sold them to singers and producers. I would go door to door to the music companies in LA and Nashville and New York City. One time my song-writing partner Fred Knipe and I wrote and sold a song called "She's Playing Hard To Forget."

The title of that song says a lot about how salespeople finally succeed. They don't stay isolated and disconnected from their clients by being cold and "professional"-acting all the time. They don't do any "hint-hint" selling. They don't play hard to get. They mix in a little human factor here and there. In the end, when the prospect has to decide between two people to give the sale to, the prospect will almost always go with the most unforgettable of the two people.

At your funeral, what made you memorable? What made you hard to forget? Sell with that.

42 Don't "Love" the Other Person, Become the Other Person

When I am interviewing someone for a sales position, the remark they make that always turns me off is, "I want to be in sales because I love people."

I usually follow that remark by saying, "Really? Hey, thanks. Good luck. Our position is already filled. Don't call us, we'll call you."

Because "loving people" in general is an empty claim. It means nothing. Nobody loves all people. It makes you sound like you are part of some kind of cult and have been hypnotized to always be friendly as a thoughtless lamb.

Liking your customer will often come quite naturally and help you in the sales process. But it isn't even necessary. What is necessary (for rapid success) is that you learn to somehow *be* your customer. To see things as she or he does. To feel life from his or her brain and body. To look at the buying process from his and her perspective. To understand everything they have experienced.

Becoming the other person is a powerful skill, and a worthy goal in your first communications. It takes commitment and a fiercely curious intelligence. It takes an ever-growing skill at questions. It takes deep listening. Listening like an industrial vacuum cleaner, taking all of that person into your mind, all their fears and hopes and thoughts.

That's the true interpersonal challenge in sales. To become the other person. Like a great actor learns to become a person. Like Will Smith learning to be Ali. It wasn't how much he liked Ali that mattered. It was whether he was willing to become Ali.

So the next time you have someone in your office who is looking for a sales position with you because they "love people," throw them out as fast as you can. You need something more real than that. You need someone more committed.

43 Reinvent Yourself

Because I have written some books on reinventing yourself, motivating yourself and living your dream, I am sometimes considered an expert by the unsuspecting.

But I have had to grow, too, while I was writing the books. I have had to reinvent myself, right along with my advising others to do so.

And the best reinvention I ever did was toward taking ownership of reality. Seizing the truth. Working with what was really there, instead of working with fuzzy dreams. Once I got clear on this subject, I tended to lose all patience with those who were not clear. It was not fair of me to flip out when people tried to sell a cloudy nebula of daydreams as the answer to real life challenges. After all, I myself used to sell the same thing. It was part of my youth. And part of my self-imposed immaturity.

Marianne was a writer for a nationally known women's magazine, and she had interviewed me a few times in the past to get quotes for articles she was doing for her magazine.

When she called again recently, she said she had already interviewed another "motivational" writer or two and wanted some quotes from me to round out the article. She wanted quotes that would support and add spice to her article's premise, but the only problem was that her article's premise ticked me off.

She had sent me an e-mail version of it with suggested areas for me to add quotes to support the concepts, but I simply couldn't support these concepts.

Take the concept of daydreaming, for example. Wasn't it a great thing for women to do? This was my response:

"I think daydreaming is infantile, and I think it's demeaning to women how many motivational speakers try to manipulate women's natural creativity by encouraging dreaming and day-dreaming and wishing and hoping. *Decide* what you want and pay the price for it. You *will* get it. Stop fooling around with daydreams and wishes and spinning around the bedpost singing his name like a bad Julie Andrews movie ... this is an insulting recommendation to women who would really like to achieve something."

You can tell I was ticked off. But so much of my own sales life had been totally stalled as I tried one New Age mystical idea after another. I wasn't in the mood anymore.

She then asked me why motivational writers talked so much about the magic of writing goals down. What, she asked, do women have to learn from this magic?

"Most women already know about this magic," I replied. "And what they know is that it is not magic. Stop trying to tell women it is magic to write your goals down. It's just sensible to do it, that's all. And of course it works. It works for the same reason it works when you write out a grocery list for a big shopping trip. It works for the same reason that it works when you call someone for directions and write the directions down instead of trying to remember them. Anything that helps the thinking process along increases the chances you will reach your goal. The more you think about your goal, the more effective your strategies are likely to be. The less you think of your goal, the less prepared you are for bringing it into reality."

She then asked me why it was part of the secret hidden wisdom of goal achievement to set a time limit for achieving your goal.

"The secret hidden wisdom is really not a secret and hardly qualifies as wisdom," I said. "Even the mentally challenged know that it makes simple sense to set a time limit. Without a specific time frame your goal is just a free-floating and endless daydream. Is your life endless? Only when you're in pain. A goal without a time frame is just a childish wish. Wishing is juvenile. It does not lead to achievement."

"Can you give me a woman's example of this?" she asked.

"When Oprah Winfrey decided she wanted to get in good enough shape to run a big-time competitive marathon," I said, "nothing actualized until she picked the exact Marine marathon in Washington DC on a specific date to get ready for. If she had said, 'a marathon someday,' she never would have run in one. The time frame is *vital*. No goal was ever made important to the human mind without one."

She then asked me about a claim I had made in one of my books that you didn't need courage to achieve your goals.

"Courage and willpower are byproducts of taking action, not qualities you need up front," I said. "Up front what you need is the actual doing of something. I suggest doing something, anything, to get moving on your goal."

"Okay," she said. "What if my goal is to fit into a size ten by Christmas?"

"To fit into a size ten by Christmas, you don't need willpower, perseverance, courage or good character," I said. "You need to take action. You need an action plan, a routine to follow, a way to track your progress, and an irrevocable decision to follow the plan. Courage is a *result* of doing these activities."

"Okay, the other self-help writers I've interviewed for the article concluded their interviews by stressing the importance of dreaming," she said. "Especially daydreaming."

By then I'd had all I could take. I myself had been seduced by a lot of this unnecessarily mysterious and wondrous magical goal-achievement wisdom over the years, but I wasn't about to sign up for it anymore.

"I think daydreaming is daydreaming," I said. "To be perfectly honest with you."

"Well, but, what about visualization?" she asked, somewhat stunned. "Don't studies show that visualization works? What about those prisoners who visualized their golf games and improved them?"

"If one of the restrictions of solitary confinement is that you can't play golf, then I think visualization just might be the last house on the block. It's all you've got! So if you're asking whether I recommend it to prisoners, I might say yes. If your magazine was *Prisoner's World* magazine, I would say yes. Please visualize all you can."

"Okay," she said. "Explain what you mean."

"It is not simply the visualization that works," I said. "It's visualization accompanied by clear, rational planning and thinking. Visualization all by itself is a New Age fraud, and my own unofficial research shows it does nothing more than get a person's hopes up. It is not a mature, effective self-confident activity … it also leads to low self-esteem. It makes you constantly focus on what you wish you had but don't. Why not focus, instead, on your next action step?"

"Okay, okay," she said. "I have a final question. Another of my self-help writers said that it was really important that you keep asking yourself a vital question."

"I bet I know what that question is," I said.

"What do you think it is?" she teased.

"I think it is the question, *To reach my goal, what else do I need to do?*"

"Actually, no," she said. "The question they recommend is, *Am I having fun?*"

My laughter took a while to cool down. For the first time in this interview, I myself was having fun.

"You've got to be kidding me," I said diplomatically.

"No," she said. "They think it's important to have fun every step of the way. And to stop often to see if you are."

"This is mere nonsense," I said.

"But the motivators say that when you're having fun you think more creatively," she said. "Don't you agree that you'll reach your goal faster if you think more creatively?"

"Yes, but thinking creatively comes from a determination to really think things through and consider all the possibilities . . . not from visualization and asking *Are we having fun yet?* Think clearly and passionately and hit your goals, and then you'll *really* be having fun."

She felt like she wasn't getting anywhere with me, so she changed the subject.

"Why does thinking with a pad work so well?" she asked. "I know it does for me. It's almost as if somebody else is doing the work and all I have to do is write the results down!"

"What?" I said. "You think your idea is coming from the great beyond? Somebody *else* is doing your good work? Look, these appeals are made especially to women who have always been taught that men are the thinkers and they should just shut up or else praise the men's brilliance. The pad works because it helps you think, obviously. Why do you use a pad to add a long list of numbers? It's not mysterious. But if you think it's not really *you* that puts the good idea down, you are suffering from low self-esteem. Who else could it be? Your imaginary friend? Some supernatural hero? Why can't it be *you* that came up with that idea?"

"Okay, okay. I get your point. I want to ask you about something I read in one of your books . . . the importance of the little things, why you think the little things, the small steps along the way are more important than the big dream?"

"Because every little achievement along the way raises our confidence. With increased confidence in ourselves, we achieve more and more. The big picture is fine, but the real success in reaching your goals is achieved when you break your plan down into small steps to take along the way, and then start taking them. With each of these steps your self-esteem rises. In the end, the goal itself isn't even as important as the huge strides you have made in self-confidence and self-respect along the way. Because of that increase in self-confidence and self-respect, the next challenge that life throws at you will be that much easier to handle. And it was those small steps that built that self-confidence."

I concluded our interview by recommending that she read *A Woman's Self-Esteem* by Nathaniel Branden and swear off the magical wisdom of New Age goal manifestation. As I have found, when you leave that "wisdom" behind, your mind becomes freed up to get you what you want in life.

44 Do Talk to Strangers

As a child you were probably told many times never to talk to strangers.

Strangers were strange. In fact, they were probably worse than strange, they were probably dangerous. They might even kill you.

Sometimes when the adult world programs us in some specific way, the programming never leaves. It gets into the patterns of our thoughts and lives there forever. We start to pick up the phone to do our cold-calling, and something stops us. We need to organize our desk first. We need to use the bathroom. It's time to grab a bite to eat.

Fear of talking to strangers can make driving around prospecting our territory more frightening than we realize. Subconsciously and subtly we put it off. Or we only do a little of it.

Or we have to rush back to the office to fax a contract.

People who have this subtle programming working against them end up twisting their sales jobs around into more difficult challenges than they need to be. They often obsess with having "contacts" in a business before calling that business. They place an exaggerated emphasis on "knowing somebody who knows somebody who knows somebody who knows Mr. Gates" rather than just calling on Mr. Gates.

You can think about things that way if you like. No one would blame you. Because it always seems nice to know people and have contacts. But the fastest way to expand your base of friends and contacts is to become absolutely fearless about calling strangers; to actually set a certain time aside each day for calling people you don't know. Calling people who don't know you from Adam. Even Mister swinging Gates.

For one thing, it will make the later-day calling of people you *do* know that much more fun and easy to do. We live by contrasts. Without the night we wouldn't experience day. Without ever feeling down, we would never enjoy feeling up.

Without the tough calls, we wouldn't know what an easy and fun call felt like.

"I'm not good at talking to people I don't know," Annie told me as we met to discuss her low cold-calling activity levels. Annie worked on a sales team that measured daily activity, especially prospecting. The team found that the more they measured it, the more of it they got.

"I bet I know why you're not good at prospecting," I said.

"I think it was my mother," she said, with a far-off look in her eye. "Or, maybe, my first couple of jobs when I felt so undertrained and rejected all the time..."

Annie's face took on the look of someone trying to remember the painful reason why this fear was in her.

"No," I said. "Nice try, but no. It's not your mother. It's not your first two jobs," I said.

"Well, how do you really know?" she asked, playfully but hiding her irritation. "Okay, let's say you do know. So what does your ego tell you you know?"

"There is no secret reason at all that you are uncomfortable making cold calls," I said. "You can keep looking for a hidden reason, but there *is* no hidden reason. There is nothing psychological that you have to try to understand. What's responsible is a number. A simple, specific number."

"What do you mean? What number?"

"Forty-seven," I said.

"Forty-seven?"

"Or maybe twenty-two, or a hundred and five," I said. "But it is a number, a specific number, and if we had a videotape of your sales life we could find that precise number and it would tell you why you don't enjoy cold-calling."

"I don't get it."

"That number is the exact number of strangers you have talked to," I said. "That is the exact number of sales conversations you have had with total strangers."

"Oh, I see. You are saying that the number represents how much practice I have had at it and practice makes perfect."

"Practice makes perfect. Yes, it does! It makes perfect pleasure, is what it makes. Not perfection per se, but a perfect, easy pleasure and grace. Practice takes your fear away and make things more and more fun to do. The problem is, it does it in such tiny, tiny increments that we don't notice the progress, so we quit."

She said, "Like when I used to try to practice the piano."

"Yes," I said. "We take up an instrument and because early practice doesn't seem to make us any better, we quit. But it is making us better. That's the point. And the more you do it, the more obvious that improvement becomes to you. But you have to do it a certain number of times. And even though I can't tell you the exact number it will be, it is a number. Looking back, it was always a certain number you hit when things got easy."

What I wanted Annie to see was that everyone on her sales staff had a number in them. If you opened the door in the back of their hearts, you could read this number as you read an odometer on a car. This number, and nothing else, would tell you how comfortable that person was talking to strangers. Or prospects.

The more strangers they had spoken to in their lives, the easier it was for them to do it today.

To speed up your success in sales, use every opportunity you can find to practice talking to strangers. The greatest soccer player of all time, Pele, was once asked, "When do you find the time to practice?"

"Everything is practice," said Pele.

When you have decided to feel the joy of becoming great at what you do, everything is practice. You can make this walk to the store a great one. You can speak to strangers along the way. You can practice being open and kind and cheerful and curious about the life of the person stocking the vegetables in the store.

My client Mariano was always living in fear of making sales presentations. His job required that he set up a display board and talk to small groups of people about his computer-learning products.

"I get terrified right before I know I have to speak in front of a group," he said. "I don't know what it is about me. Maybe an experience in grade school. Once in grade school I had to give a book report and halfway through I realized my fly was open. But I didn't know that at the beginning. Everyone was laughing at me. I wanted to go home and die. I asked my mom if I could go to another school."

"What have you done about it?" I asked him.

"Everything I can think of," he said. "I even went to a therapist, and he gave me some medication, little yellow pills, and I didn't feel as afraid when I used them, but I didn't feel in control, either. Once, a week after a presentation, I found out that my customer thought I was rambling incoherently. He said I was slurring my words and talking so slowly that no one could understand me. That was not rewarding. I don't use the pills anymore."

I knew right away how to put my finger on the reason why Mariano was uncomfortable in front of groups. It wasn't anything deeply wounded in his psyche (although the book report with the fly down in grade school could not have helped).

It was a number.

It was the specific number of times he had done it. That was responsible for his fear. Because, as Emerson so loved to say, "Courage is having done it before."

Because of the traumatic memory in grade school, Mariano had probably subconsciously kept that number as low as he could throughout his life. And the lower the number, the higher the anxiety.

"You must run some clicks on that number," I said. "Even if you have to do it artificially at first. A number is a number, and only the number can save you."

"What do you mean by artificially?"

"Give the presentation to your wife," I said. "A number of times. Have your family come over to see it. Give it to your friends at work. Ask them if you can do it for all of them after a sales meeting. Do it again and again and again. Click, click, click, click. And when the clicks tumble your numbers up to the right levels, watch the joy sneak into your presentations."

Some people spend their whole lives not talking to strangers.

It does not give them a safer life. It only keeps their number and their happiness down way low.

45 Go Nonlinear

Sometimes it's fun and profitable, after you've gotten good at hitting singles, to pick a day to go nonlinear on yourself. To make a total quantum leap, not from A to B, but from A to infinity.

In other words, sometimes it's very effective to go crazy for a while and do things normal salespeople would never dream of doing. To think big and ask for a huge price and a major deal. Just to see the look on their faces.

Normal salespeople are often very linear. They go from A to B to C to D to E to F to G. They are incremental all day, all week, all month, all year. They make continuous improvements, little by little, inching their way from being miserable to being little better than miserable. Baby steps. All in a row.

You ought to try breaking out of this routine every so often. Change how you sell completely. Just for a thrill. Just to see how fun and crazy you can make your sales life be.

And always keep in mind that your sales life has the potential—more potential, actually, than just about any other profession—to be fun and crazy.

That's because one of the great things about sales is that there is no right way to always do it well. You can do it many different ways. Experiments will succeed at opening you up to more and more possibilities. The possibilities are almost infinite.

On one sales call I went on, I took my guitar.

I sang my prospective customer a song. It was the fight song from the University of Arizona called "Bear Down, Arizona!" I knew he loved the Arizona Wildcats. We had joked about it on one of our first calls. My song showed him that I am not someone who forgets those calls.

One day, later in my life, I gave a talk to a sales staff in which I told them to slow down and take their time. The next month I told the same staff to speed everything up! I told them to live each day this week as if it were their last day before a long vacation, and they had to close everything!

They said, "Are you nuts? You told us last week to slow down."

My point was to shake things up. The brain plays dead when it's left alone with no new thinking.

46 Agree with Every Feeling

It was cold-calling time for me one day in my office at my seminar-training company a few years ago, and I was on the telephone with a man named Gary who was the general manager of a large car dealership in Phoenix. I had done some very successful seminars with one of Gary's associated dealerships recently, and was trying to sell Gary on the idea that I could do some for him as well.

Unfortunately, he wasn't buying.

"If you worked for them, I don't even want to talk to you," he said.

"Really?" I said, very surprised that the dealership I mentioned didn't impress him.

"Their culture is so different from ours, their leadership is so different from mine, that if you worked for them I know I can't use you."

I was getting the point that Gary hated these guys I had worked for. So I knew the time was not right for arguing with that feeling.

Because I had to learn the hard way long ago that the time is *never* right to argue with a feeling. Not if I wanted a sale. Too many people in this world try to make other people's feelings wrong. They try to talk people out of what they are feeling. It not only doesn't work, but it causes people to dig in deeper. They become even more defensive, and they defend the logic of their feelings.

Every feeling anyone has ever felt has been the right feeling at that time for that person. It's also the exact feeling you would have if you were that person. Yet I'm amazed, constantly, at how many people try to talk other people out of their feelings.

"You shouldn't feel that way," they say. "You have no reason to feel that way."

But a feeling is just a feeling. It's just like a fever. It is felt in the body, like a fever. It can't be right or wrong (like a judgment) because it's just a feeling. You would never tell someone they shouldn't have the fever that they have.

"You have nothing to base that fever on," is not something you would say.

So I treated Gary's feeling like it was right. Whatever it was, it was right. I had long ago learned to agree with how my buyers feel. Their feelings are right. About everything. Their reasoning may not be right, but what they feel is what they feel.

"I can see how you would feel that way," I laughed. "It's pretty obvious to me that you feel completely different from that other dealership, and that my seminar wouldn't be a fit for you at all!"

"That's absolutely right," said Gary. "And I don't mean to insult you. I just don't want to waste your time. I like to be up-front."

"I respect that," I said. "But now you've really got me interested. I'd love to know in what ways you're different from that dealership, because I know you are really successful and so are they. It really interests me. Just for my own education, would you mind if I came by and you told me about how you do things over there? I thought the other dealership couldn't be improved on …"

"Well, you're wrong about that!" said Gary. "I would rather be broke and homeless than to do business like they do, so if you think they are great then you don't know a lot about car sales."

"Obviously not," I said.

"Okay," he said. "Come over today at about four. I'll talk to you. I'll educate you. I'll tell you how we do business here."

I was very pleased when I hung up the phone. I had gone from being completely rejected to being invited over.

Sitting down in Gary's office was one of the best sales experiences of my life. We talked for over an hour about the differences between his dealership and the other one. He was very proud of his systems and I agreed that they were impressive and effective. During the talk with Gary we stayed focused for the whole time on his systems and experiences and successes. I didn't once bring up my seminars.

But I left his dealership with a check in my hand, made out to me!

When we were through talking, I thanked him and stood up to leave. He asked me to wait a second. He had a question.

"So, you're a good seminar leader?" he said.

"Yes," I said.

"Well, I'll tell you what. I'm going to try you out. Just to see if you're a fit for us. You seem to understand my system pretty well. And to tell you the truth, I had heard about you from the other dealership. If you promise you'll keep your talks pointed to my basic ways, I'll give you a try. How much do you cost?"

I gave him a price for day-of-presentation, and a slightly reduced price for prepayment. He reached into a file drawer and pulled out a huge checkbook. He wrote me a check on the spot.

As I drove home, I realized that I had not disagreed with anything Gary had felt, including his feeling that I was inappropriate for his dealership. And that's why I had the check.

47 Become a True Believer

I got a call yesterday from Mark, a sales manager working on his second year of leading the nation in sales.

"I find that when I'm in my game or at my best, sometimes called 'the zone,' it feels like I'm in rhythm," he said.

"Tell me what you mean," I said, always anxious to learn from someone who leads the nation in sales.

"The rhythm is almost a spiritual feeling," Mark said. "And it actually energizes you to sell even more. The rhythm is hard to describe except that it comes from inside your chest and every contact with a customer seems to be a winning one and you think that you are having a great day."

"Can you keep that rhythm going all the time?" I asked.

"No!" he said. "That's the problem. Because we are human it is easy to break out of this rhythm and become out of sync with the sales process. The more out of sync we are, the worse it gets and the longer it lasts. Being out of sync can occur because of a loss of confidence, a long vacation, being sick, losing a big deal, or really any outside event that tricks your mind into worrying or losing focus."

"What do you mean by tricking your mind?" I said. "Those outside events are real, aren't they?"

"Of course they are real, but what you think about them is always made-up," he said. "The real key to sales is knowing that you are free. Free to think anything you want. I can think a vacation has pulled me out of sync, or I can think it has totally refreshed me and made me ready to jump back in and enjoy the ride."

"Once you do jump back in, how do you jump-start that rhythm again?"

"The best salespeople know how to get into their own rhythm," he said. "Each person's technique is different. But when you understand yours and know when you are in it and when you are not, you have reached enlightenment. The reason I use the word 'enlightenment' is that you start to become aware of your own sales process and therefore can get into rhythm on your own without outside influences."

"How does the rhythm show itself?"

"I have found that rhythm is a combination of things: relationship building, product knowledge, confidence, and motivation. Once these are all in sync, then you can sell anything, like the proverbial statement, 'He can sell snow to the Eskimos.'"

"And getting out of your rhythm is like losing your religion?"

"Literally. You become a nonbeliever, so you're just going through the motions. The rhythm is contained in your faith in your product. Your excitement about it."

"What is the role of your sales manager in all of this?" I asked.

"A great sales manager has one job: to turn his own people into believers. True believers can sell anything. They don't need a technique."

I thought my conversation with Mark was significant, because it helped me understand some of the successes I have had with salespeople who were stuck in mediocre performance. I realized that I especially enjoyed helping people who have not found that rhythm yet.

And I think Mark revealed a major secret when he advocated "product knowledge," how to completely fall in love with what your product can do for someone. Once that excitement takes over, you can talk to anybody about it. Therefore I think the rhythm must be accessed through product knowledge (step one) followed by many good conversations (step two).

When you go on vacation, that's exactly what you lose, that intimate product knowledge. You forget it. So it's hard to get back on the phone. To say that you have "lost your rhythm" is true. But that's too mysterious for a new salesperson to hear. That "rhythm" has to be something anyone can get back into.

When you come back from a long vacation, take the time to immerse yourself in your product again. You'll feel that rhythm coming back, and the joy that accompanies it.

48 Look for Trust

Patricia was a person who was not popular in high school. From that time on she resented the whole idea of popularity and being liked.

Now that she was in sales, she was becoming even more bitter about the whole idea of being liked by people.

"My belief for the moment is that people will find a way to buy from you if they *like you* as a person more than who they are currently doing business with," she said. "If they don't like you, you are out of luck."

I agreed with her to a point. But I thought there was more to liking you than just superficially enjoying you.

"I just lost a big sale," she said. "And I'm really depressed about it. They just liked the other person better. Nothing more than that."

"Never base any conclusion on one experience," I said. "You can interpret that loss of sale any way you want. But in the long run, there is a lot more to selling than just the superficiality of being liked."

I wanted Patricia to realize that most people, in fact, base their sales decisions on trust. Not whether you have a pleasing personality or are high-school-type "popular." But rather it's *trust* based on what they see as your commitment.

For example, I *like* the guy who cleans my yard because of his huge commitment to serve me. To do a good job for me. To "take good care" of me. Anyone with any personality whatsoever can outperform anyone else in this category with a simple commitment to do so.

"You're talking about something else," Patricia said. "You're talking about what happens *after* they become your customer. I agree with you that it's easy after ... you just focus on service."

"Then what are you talking about?" I asked her.

"What I am referring to is *before* they are my customer. I'm talking about getting people to *become* my customer. That's where I'm beginning to think it's all based on how likable you are."

I saw the trap Patricia had set for herself with this subject. So I tried a different idea to try to get her to see that it isn't just about being liked.

"Patricia," I said. "I once worked with a salesperson who lost a ton of business because all he knew how to be was likable. He was one of those happy smiling fraternity-boy types. He never did his homework, he just laughed and smiled and kept being likable. The only problem was that there were many times when his clients wanted a serious businessperson to deal with, a *committed* person who made serious efforts to truly help. He turned off a lot of people, and the more important the person he dealt with, the bigger the turn-off he was. Whenever they asked him a complex question about how their own business would employ his product, he engaged in inappropriate laughter and joking."

Patricia was a serious, studious salesperson. So her "weakness" was her strength. I wanted her to stay with it and stay focused on the outcomes she wanted and forget the few she lost. Especially the ones she lost when stupid grins bonded with stupid grins.

"Be yourself, Patricia, be committed to your result, and win," I said. "In the long run, you will win."

Her smile when she heard those words made her look very likable to me.

49 You Already Know How to Succeed

Toning up your physical figure and toning up your sales figures reveal the same secret to success. And it's a secret you already know about down deep in your mind.

Are you heavier than you want to be? Deep down you know that what you have is a math problem, not a weight problem. Deep down you already know that you won't lose weight until you realize that human fat has a number on it. Yes, fat is numerical even more than it is physical.

Are you not selling what you want to? Sales success has a number, too. And when you learn how to bring that number into crystal focus, your sales will come to you.

Deep down inside you already know this. There's a math equation to success that you have known about since you were a small child.

Because I make my living as a human performance coach, there has been one key observation revealed to me over and over again: The clients who have the most dramatic successes are fanatical about their numbers. When I come in to do a training project, they know the numbers that are being produced and they know the target numbers they want to reach.

When they ask me to help them reach their target numbers, I agree to. I know what to teach them and I know what to teach their salespeople. Although what I teach is something they already subconsciously knew. (They just didn't always know that they knew it.)

Most of the thinking in society today goes against the mathematical formula for success. Most of the thinking tells you that your environment is largely responsible for your numbers. It tells you that circumstances are responsible for your numbers. Society will place exaggerated importance on the mercurial whims of other people as a direct influence on your numbers.

But this is not reality. What's true is that you yourself are what moves your numbers.

When you get a grip on that reality, you have new power to perform at levels you had not performed at before.

That simple reality is hard to grip. Believe me. It keeps slipping away. Like a tiny fish you are trying to capture in the water with your hand.

Let's look at what society's thinking does to disconnect people from their power to change their numbers. We all have numbers. People who work directly with their numbers succeed. People who hide their numbers, disown their numbers, or simply avoid their numbers fail.

I recently came across an article in a major news magazine about obesity in America. The basic theme was that increased obesity is being caused by the environment and circumstances and the greedy whims of other people. Too much fast food is now too available for us not to become obese. The meals are now too big. The drinks are larger than they used to be. The burgers are absolutely huge. Supersizing fools us into trying to be cost-conscious while doubling and tripling the calories that are being secretly slipped into us. That was the point of the article.

But fat has a number attached to it. Human fat is numerical. It's not some vague immeasurable amorphous blob of misery. It's a number.

The math of fat is a simple one. (Just as the math of a bad sales month is a simple one, as is the math of a batting slump.) The math of fat says that the food you eat has a number on it. That number is calories. The math of physical activity has a number on it too. That number is calories *burned*. (For example, you burn more calories standing up than you do sitting down.) It is a mathematical certainty (confirmed in studies with humans and laboratory animals for decades now) that when you reduce the calories going in, and/or increase the calories going out (being burned up by exercise), you lose weight.

It's a numbers game.

Deep down, people already know this. Deep down they always knew it was about numbers. Because when something hugely important, or a big crisis comes up, people always go right to the numbers. When their phone is about to be disconnected because they missed a payment, they go right to the exact numbers. When they're serious about a result, they work with numbers.

Let's imagine that I weigh 210 pounds, and someone tells me that I will be paid a million dollars to have a simple part in a movie filming in my home town, but I have to weigh 180 to be in the movie. They say if I report on the set at 180 I'll get a million in cash on the spot and I'll shoot three scenes with Meg Ryan.

What do I do? Do I say, "That will be impossible because of super-sizing"? I can't do that because an order of fries today is larger than it used to be?

No. I want to be in this movie. So I weigh myself, first off. That's a number. That's reality. That's where I really am. Then I make a list of foods and their caloric numbers. Then I make a list of exercises and their caloric numbers. I chart a plan. Numbers in, numbers out. I measure the progress of my plan every day. If I have to adjust my plan, I do. I am definitely going to collect that money and be on the set with Meg Ryan.

I have free will, and the choice is mine.

(If the number of calories you have consumed in any given day were printed out as a number on your forehead at all times, so that everywhere you went people could see the exact number, would that number be likely to go down? Almost everyone says an emphatic yes to this.)

Charting and measuring "Numbers in / Numbers out" looks like a simple and logical plan, the kind of plan that you would tell anyone to do.

But most people in today's society would scoff at that plan. Let's look at that article I read on obesity in America.

The article, in *U.S. News & World Report*, first reports that a recent Harvard survey showed that two out of three people said the obesity epidemic could be explained by overweight people "lacking willpower" to diet and exercise. Sounds logical.

Would you agree with that? I think I would if you added a vital component: that they lacked the desire and commitment to create a numerically accountable plan to lose weight. (If you want to find out if something is a really big priority in someone's life, simply find out if they are charting it and measuring it.)

But the Harvard survey results that said people "lacked willpower" to lose weight were scoffed at and mocked by the experts. According to the University of Colorado nutrition expert James Hill, that simple conclusion is nonsense! Nonsense!

As James Hill puts it, "Our physiology tells us to eat whenever food is available. And now, food is *always* available."

Our physiology also tells us to urinate when our bladders are full. But does that mean we do? Always? Not exactly. In fact, we almost always find a restroom first. To say that we must get fat because of all the food that's now available is like saying we must walk around with our clothing soaked because of how many times our physiology tells us we have to urinate.

Our physiology tells us a lot of things. But do we always give our

STEVE CHANDLER

physiology the last word? Not unless we're infants. If we are grown up, we have functional minds, too. Minds that were designed to pronounce the last word. And that's something modern society seems to want to leave out of the equation.

"The way society is today," says Hill, "the only way most people can maintain a healthy weight is with active cognitive control—that is, they're thinking about it most of the time." The problem, he adds, is that few people have the skills necessary to balance how much they're eating against the calories they're using up in physical activity.

Skills?

What skills are those? What skills are necessary to be aware of how much you are eating? What skills are needed for you to be aware of how much you are moving around?

There are only two factors here: what you are putting in your mouth, and how much you are moving your body. What special skills are needed to be aware of those two factors?

The experts believe you need skills that you don't have. Skills that maybe government programs can teach you. Or expensive obesity clinics. But what are these secret skills?

The skill of awareness. The skill of commitment. Skills you have known how to use since you were six years old.

And what about this sophisticated activity the nutrition expert identified as "active cognitive control"? Would we really have to learn to do something as complex-sounding as that? "Active cognitive control" is one of those modern terms meant to get you to write a check. You may be writing it to an expensive treatment center or to the IRS as you are taxed for a complicated government program. "Active cognitive control" is actually a very simple thing. In a word, it is *focus*.

When you *stay focused* on what needs to be done, you will almost always achieve your goal. And for the human mind to clearly focus, numbers need to be at the forefront. Activity needs to move to the beat of those numbers. If you consistently do this, you will solve your problems. You will reach your goals.

But don't ever forget to bring out the numbers. Spread them across the table and study them. Without the numbers, you won't know where you are. And you won't know where to go next.

Let's look again at obesity. If I take full responsibility for everything that I put into my mouth, I am off to a good start. If I then take full responsibility for how much I move my body around, I am building the foundation for success. Finally, and most important, if I take full responsibility for putting precise numerical measurement at the top of my awareness, then I am home free. What needs to be done is clear and simple.

The same is true in sales. The same is true in any business's revenue. Certain things increase revenue, certain things don't.

The best coaches in the world have a simple formula. They want to see the numbers. They study the activities that created those numbers. They figure out what needs to be done to hit more of those numbers. They then teach people to focus on *what needs to be done.*

It sounds painfully simple, but most people don't do it. They focus on other things, almost at random. They focus on other people. They focus on what other people think of them. They focus on their resentments. They focus on their self-doubts. They focus on their childhood issues. They do not focus on what needs to be done.

Eaters who do not lose weight are simply not focusing on what needs to be done. They are focused on what they *feel like doing.*

People failing at work do the same thing. If I'm feeling guilt or anxiety or anything unpleasant, I then focus on what might change this feeling. A chat with a friend? A visit to an entertaining website? A trip to the coffee and cookie room? An angry, lengthy e-mail to some other department in the company, just to get this feeling off my chest? How about an early movie in the name of going "into the field" for the rest of the day?

After a long enough period of doing these mood-altering activities, I think something is wrong. I need some special new training to sell more. Maybe someone can come in and teach me Active Cognitive Control! Maybe they have treatment centers for chronic underachievers. Or, even better, government programs.

They probably will someday. But the best ones will end up teaching you what you already knew at age six. If you want something, focus on it. Focus on it until you get it.

50 Gather Mentors and Use Them

Collect advisors, mentors, consultants, coaches and heroes in the field of sales. Find out who the top salesperson is in one of your customers' businesses and take her (or him) to lunch.

The more you talk to people who have succeeded in sales, the faster you yourself will succeed. Don't operate in a vacuum of ignorance. Open yourself up to all kinds of help.

Get advice from other salespeople on your team. Learn everything about the top salespeople. Learn how they do it. If you do what they do, you will succeed, too.

Let your manager mentor you, too. Chances are she or he has succeeded big-time at what you may be struggling with. Let them take you on as a pet project.

All of this involves a commitment. A decision. The decision is this: You are going to learn to be great. Not good, but great.

So learn everything you can from the greats.

If you have a distant cousin in sales halfway across the country, call him. Ask a million questions. Get interested. Get excited. Take sales up as a hobby. Become absolutely fascinated by how so many people do it so many different ways. Learn all those ways.

Most fear is fear of the unknown. We only fear what we don't understand. If we're not quite sure how the process of sales works, we will feel anxiety all the time. Remove that fear by increasing your understanding. The more you learn, the more you'll earn. Don't go halfway.

People often lose their marriages by not being fully committed to the marriage and the other person. They're married, but they're not sure they want to completely commit, so they still look around, even while they are married. When we see people like this on soap operas, we call them sleazeballs. They are the evil characters in the soap opera, never committing to anything.

Don't be sleazy about your profession. Don't run it down or complain about it at home. Your profession is pure opportunity. Either commit to it completely, or move on. But I promise you, once you really commit, a burden will be lifted. You'll be free to enjoy yourself.

51 Make Your Sale Right Now

"What was your major in college?" I asked a prospective client once while visiting his office and seeing a number of college degrees framed on his walls.

"Oceanography," he said.

Where do you go with that one? How do you talk knowledgeably about that? I didn't know, but I kept talking because I wanted to stay with him in the friendship-building process.

"I love the ocean," I said. "And due to my personal interest in the ocean, I've spent many hours viewing the TV program *Baywatch*."

My client just stared at me. Then he burst out laughing.

(Victor Borge said, "The shortest distance between two people is a laugh." And in building sales relationships it is fun to make it fun. The joy of selling is in the fun you can bring to it.)

To me the beauty of humor is that it signals for sure that there is not linear time, just as one does not accumulate a linear tapeworm life. I know in my soul that linear time is a human invention. We use it to measure activities. We use it so that we can show up with the right people at the first tee on the golf course.

But in reality, there is no linear time. One is presented with a series of fresh moments, each one containing all of time.

This is a fresh moment right now.

About the Author

Steve Chandler is a sales consultant and public speaker whose clients include Merrill Lynch, Motorola, Checker Auto, M&I Banks, Honeywell, and many more.

He is the author of the best-selling books and audio series *Reinventing Yourself, 100 Ways to Motivate Yourself, RelationShift,* and *17 Lies That Are Holding You Back and the Truth That Will Set You Free.*

Internationally sought-after as a public speaker, Chandler has been called by PBS, "an insane combination of Jerry Seinfeld and Anthony Robbins."

Information about sales training and consulting from Steve Chandler can be obtained from Stephen Chandler Incorporated at 480-892-6290 or 100Ways@Compuserve.com.

Books Available From Robert D. Reed Publishers

Please include payment with orders. Send indicated book/s to:

Name:_____

Address:_____

City:_____ State:_____ Zip:_____

Phone:(_____)_____ E-mail:_____

Titles and Authors	Unit Price
_____ *The Joy of Selling: Breakthrough ideas that lead to success in sales* by Steve Chandler	$11.95
_____ *RelationShift: Revolutionary Fundraising* by Michael Bassoff and Steve Chandler	$14.95
_____ *The Ten Commitments to Your Success* by Steve Chandler	$11.95
_____ *Gotta Minute? The ABC's of Successful Living* by Tom Massey, Ph.D., N.D.	9.95
_____ *Gotta Minute? Practical Tips for Abundant Living: The ABC's of Total Health* by Tom Massey, Ph.D., N.D.	9.95
_____ *Gotta Minute? How to Look & Feel Great!* by Marcia F. Kamph, M.S., D.C.	11.95
_____ *Gotta Minute? Yoga for Health, Relaxation & Well-being* by Nirvair Singh Khalsa	9.95
_____ *Gotta Minute? Ultimate Guide of One-Minute Workouts for Anyone, Anywhere, Anytime!* by Bonnie Nygard, M.Ed. & Bonnie Hopper, M.Ed.	9.95

Enclose a copy of this order form with payment for books. Send to the address below. Shipping & handling: $2.50 for first book plus $1.00 for each additional book. California residents add 8.5% sales tax. We offer discounts for large orders.

Please make checks payable to: **Robert D. Reed Publishers.**

Total enclosed: $_____. See our website for more books!

Robert D. Reed Publishers
P.O. Box 1992, Bandon, OR 97411
Phone: 541-347-9882 • Fax: 541-347-9883
Email: 4bobreed@msn.com • www.rdrpublishers.com